# YOU'LL NEVER GET LOST AGAIN

## SIMPLE NAVIGATION FOR EVERYONE

---

### REVISED 2ND EDITION

BY CAPTAIN ROBERT R. SINGLETON PHD

# YOU'LL NEVER GET LOST AGAIN: SIMPLE NAVIGATION FOR EVERYONE

1405 SW 6th Avenue • Ocala, Florida 34471 • Phone 800-814-1132 • Fax 352-622-1875
Website: www.atlantic-pub.com • Email: sales@atlantic-pub.com
SAN Number: 268-1250

Library of Congress Cataloging-in-Publication Data

Names: Singleton, Robert Randolph, 1937- author.
Title: You'll never get lost again : simple navigation for everyone / by Captain Robert R. Singleton, PhD.
Other titles: You will never get lost again | Simple navigation
Description: Second Edition. | Ocala, Florida : Atlantic Publishing Group, Inc., [2018] | Previous edition published: New York : Winchester Press, [1979] | Includes bibliographical references and index.
Identifiers: LCCN 2018010865 (print) | LCCN 2018012656 (ebook) | ISBN 9781620235911 (ebook) | ISBN 9781620235904 (paperback : alk. paper) | ISBN 1620235900 (paperback : alk. paper)
Subjects: LCSH: Orienteering. | Navigation.
Classification: LCC GV200.4 (ebook) | LCC GV200.4 .S64 2018 (print) | DDC 796.58—dc23
LC record available at https://lccn.loc.gov/2018010865

Printed in the United States

PROJECT MANAGER: Danielle Lieneman
INTERIOR LAYOUT AND JACKET DESIGN: Nicole Sturk

# Reduce. Reuse.
# RECYCLE.

A decade ago, Atlantic Publishing signed the Green Press Initiative. These guidelines promote environmentally friendly practices, such as using recycled stock and vegetable-based inks, avoiding waste, choosing energy-efficient resources, and promoting a no-pulping policy. We now use 100-percent recycled stock on all our books. The results: in one year, switching to post-consumer recycled stock saved 24 mature trees, 5,000 gallons of water, the equivalent of the total energy used for one home in a year, and the equivalent of the greenhouse gases from one car driven for a year.

*Over the years, we have adopted a number of dogs from rescues and shelters. First there was Bear and after he passed, Ginger and Scout. Now, we have Kira, another rescue. They have brought immense joy and love not just into our lives, but into the lives of all who met them.*

*We want you to know a portion of the profits of this book will be donated in Bear, Ginger and Scout's memory to local animal shelters, parks, conservation organizations, and other individuals and nonprofit organizations in need of assistance.*

**– Douglas & Sherri Brown,**
**President & Vice-President of Atlantic Publishing**

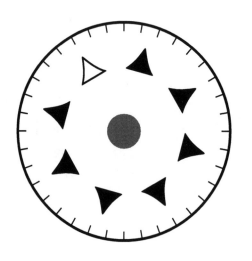

# FOREWORD

"You'll Never Get Lost Again: Simple Navigation for Everyone," was first published several decades ago, sometime after Columbus but before all the new scientific technology came about.

Today with orbiting satellites, GPS-global positioning systems, tracking software, and heaven knows what else, it would seem the old methods of navigation should have been dismissed as relics of the Stone Age long ago. However, dear Reader, believe me, they are not. While most people rely on the accuracy, speed, and ease of use that the new systems afford them, they lose sight of the basic science and pure accuracy of how to get from one place to another.

Now, here's the rub: what happens when the satellites fail or the transmitters fall silent? This is when common sense, a small magnetic compass, and perhaps a map become the basic tools of the trade. Learning how to use these items will give you knowledge and confidence in an adverse situation. This information may very well save your, or some else's, life one day.

Captain Robert R. Singleton, PhD

# DEDICATION

To Napoleon Bonaparte, Emperor of France

I dedicate this work to the great Corsican for the reason made apparent in the following short story. I have no way of knowing whether the story is true or not, but the idea it expresses is what is important.

*Marshal Ney, the great firebrand of France, paced back and forth before his Emperor's desk. Napoleon seemed unimpressed by his first Marshal's nervous and upset condition. "Please hear me," Ney pleaded. Napoleon studied a map of Russia with jaundiced eye.*

*"My dear Ney, calm yourself."*

*"But, Emperor, this man DeFarge whom you have made a general is the dumbest man in all of France."*

*"Yes, isn't it wonderful?"*

*"But, but this man is a joke, a baboon, a turkey."*

*"Yes," agreed Napoleon calmly, "it took us years to find such a man. We searched the country over and he was carefully chosen."*

*"But, Worship, you have made him a full general on your staff and he's an idiot."*

*"I agree," said Napoleon. "He is an idiot, but he is also one of the most important men in my Empire."*

*"But why?" asked Ney, completely baffled. "Why?"*

*The Emperor waited a long silent moment for his Marshal to regain his composure. "When I give an order," he said, at last, "I always give it in the presence of this man DeFarge. I state my orders simply so that DeFarge can understand them. And if DeFarge can understand my instructions, there is no excuse for anyone else not to."*

*Well, we all know what happened. Napoleon was exiled. Ney was executed. As for DeFarge, legend has it that he somehow escaped to America, married, changed his name, and fathered fifteen children whose descendants are involved in politics to this very day.*

# TABLE OF CONTENTS

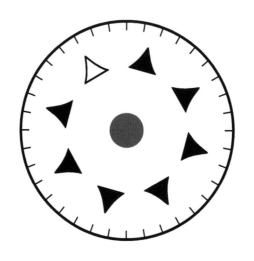

# YOU'LL NEVER GET LOST AGAIN

## SIMPLE NAVIGATION FOR EVERYONE

—

# CHAPTER 1

# UNDERSTANDING NAVIGATION AND DIRECTION

Stated simply, navigation is the science of getting yourself or your vehicle from one place to another. Here's an example of how the science works:

Get out of your chair, go into the kitchen, get yourself a beer or what have you, and return to your chair.

You have simply managed to navigate and perform several automatic actions on your outward and return trips:

1. You chose a destination.

2. You followed *reference points* to get to that destination.

3. You traveled at a certain speed.

4. It took you a specific length of time to reach your destination. Once you were there, you reversed direction and returned to your original starting point.

Now, let's look at the factors involved:

- Objective

- Direction

- Distance

- Speed

- Time

All these factors are at play whenever we move from one place to another, whether it's to the refrigerator, across the ocean, or to the corner grocery store.

Let's have a look at the path you traveled to get to the kitchen from your chair.

You can see by the path line that you changed your direction three times because of obstacles in your way. Had there been no obstacles your path line would have looked like this:

The distance you traveled would have been less and, assuming you used the same speed as before, your traveling time would have been shorter.

Now let's look at those obstacles. You were familiar with the location of each one and each was a reference point that you used on your journey toward your objective.

This is the simplest form of navigation: following one known reference point to another until you reach your destination. We spend all our lives doing this. When we go to the grocery store, to the post office, or simply to the mailbox. It is when we lose sight of an objective and have no familiar reference points to guide us that we lose direction, or, in other words, get lost.

There are so many navigational devices available today to help us keep our sense of direction. Some are simple, almost foolproof, and easy to understand, while others are extremely complicated and are mainly used by professionals. Later on in this book, we will touch briefly on those more complicated aids and explain their functions.

However, in my 50 years as a skipper, airplane pilot, and backwoods brush-buster, I have found that the simple aids are usually best. In several cases I'm familiar with, the more complicated method or instrument failed. It was the old, easy-to-use stand-by that got the person back to the barn. Therefore, it's the simple methods and tools that we will cover in detail.

Not too long ago, during an introduction to a course in Basic Navigation I teach at Hampshire College in Amherst, Massachusetts, one of my students asked, "What is the most important tool in navigation?"

I put the question back to the class and the answer came quickly from a young Nova Scotian whose family spends their lives at sea. "Common sense," he said smiling. And, without a doubt, he was absolutely right. After talking to people who have been involved in several hundred search and rescue operations at sea, I have found that common sense is the most neglected and most important navigational tool of them all.

## THE DIRECTION CIRCLE

We're going to have to get you out of your chair again. Stand up and face an object, let's say your mother-in-law's picture on the wall. Now, slowly turn yourself clockwise from the same spot in a complete circle, stopping where you started. You have just faced 360 different directions in which you could have traveled, provided there were no barriers or obstacles in your way.

No matter where you are or what's around you, you always have those 360 directions, or degrees, to choose from which to travel. And, remember, even as you move, you still have a circle measuring 360 degrees around you.

The top of this circle (where you started and stopped your turn), at the 360-degree mark and zero-degree mark, we'll label north. The very bottom (halfway through your turn), at the 180-degree mark, we'll mark south. And on the right-hand side, exactly at the 90-degree mark, is east. Its opposite, on the left-hand side at 270 degrees is west.

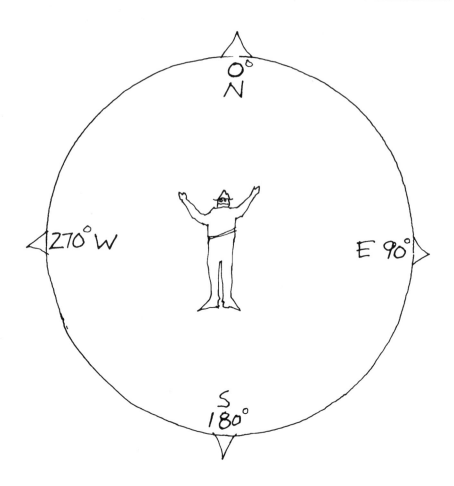

These are the four major directions; north is the most important, and you'll see why soon.

Now let's look at the 45-degree mark between north and east. This is northeast. (Doesn't that bring back memories of old sea movies? *Bring her to the Nor'east, Mr. Christian.*)

Now that you get the gist of it, it should be easy for you to locate southeast, southwest, and northwest there at the 135-, 225-, and 315-degree marks, respectively.

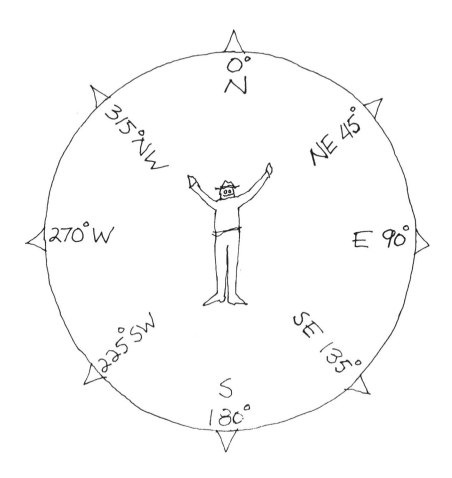

What we have done so far is label degrees of your circle of movement as directions. We can do this further by splitting the difference between the ones we have now. In this way, you can now locate north northeast, and north northwest, and so on. When we start cutting directions any finer, I prefer to use numerical degree designations instead. That way there is less chance of making a mistake.

COMPASS CARD SHOWING ALL POINTS
OF COMPASS AND ALL DEGREES

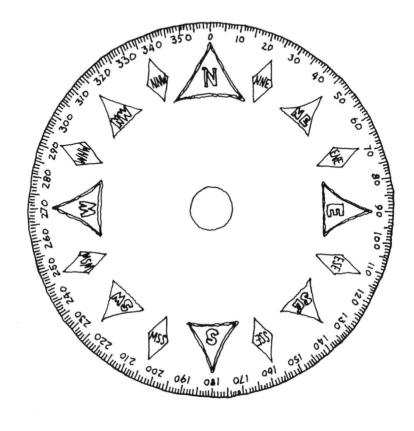

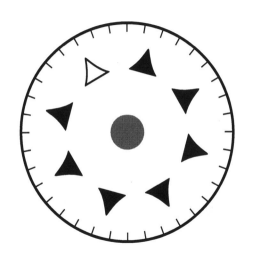

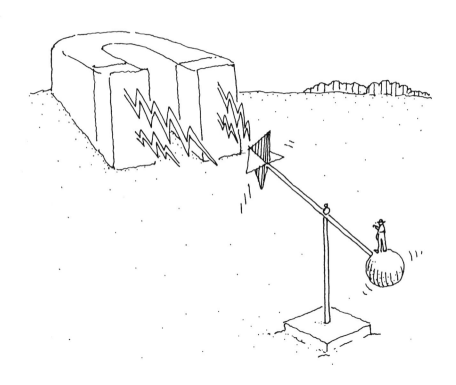

# CHAPTER 2

# THE MAGNETIC COMPASS

Now that you understand degrees and the directions they represent, let's go back to that picture on the wall that we used as a beginning point from which to start our circle.

Remember what we said about always being in the middle of a circle with 360 directions to choose from no matter where we are? Well, for us to keep those directions in the same place, no matter where we move, we need a mark, or beginning point, that will not change.

This is what a *magnetic compass* has: it always points north, and this is why north is the most important direction. A magnetic compass is a small magnetized needle or wheel that is attracted to a large magnetic deposit near the North Pole. Of all the tools used in navigation, the magnetic compass is the simplest, and one of the most important ever developed by man.

The average hand-held magnetic compass consists of a magnetized needle, a compass card (a circle with the degrees and directions printed on it, with which you are now familiar), a post, and a case made of nonmagnetic material.

The magnetized needle is suspended from the center post and swings freely enabling it to find north. This swinging motion is called *homing*. Most well-made, hand-held compasses (and many marine compasses), are liquid-filled, with either alcohol or mineral oil solutions. This helps slow the homing action and steadies the needle to make the compass easier to read.

## THE MAGNETIC COMPASS

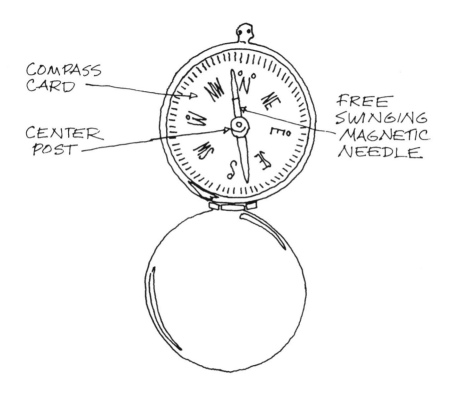

The marine compass is a little different in construction, but still performs the same essential function of showing you in which direction magnetic north lies.

If you are planning a trip and you haven't already purchased a compass, you should do so at once. You can find them at prices varying from $8.00 and upwards, but $10.00 should buy a pretty good instrument. I paid $3.50 for mine, but that was back when gas was 28¢ a gallon!

Try to find one with a *direction arrow*; that's a small needle that you can set to any degree that you want to remember or follow.

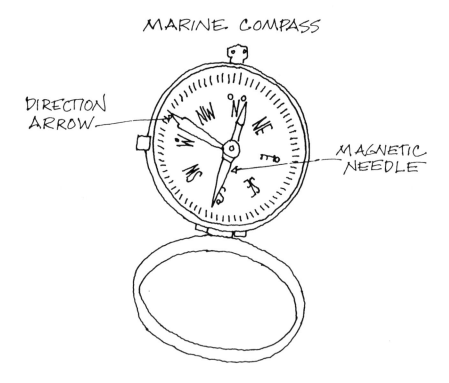

MARINE COMPASS

DIRECTION ARROW

MAGNETIC NEEDLE

Also, if you spend a lot of time in open country, you may want a *lensatic compass*, which has an attachment similar to a gun sight, so that you can look through it, take a sighting on a distant object, and get a direction reading at the same time.

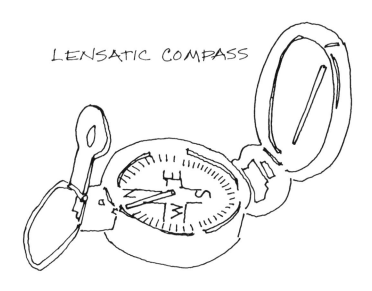

If you own a boat and plan to spend time on the water, there is no substitute for a good, dependable marine compass. You should be prepared to spend a few extra dollars to buy a really good one; your life and the lives of your family and friends, not to mention the survival of both your boat and equipment, may depend on it.

However, the best, most expensive compass in existence still isn't worth a damn if you don't know how to read it.

In the summer of 1972, I was out bass fishing in Cape Cod Bay when I received a radio call to be on the lookout for a 26-foot sailboat that had been missing for a little over two days. As fortune would have it, we located this boat about 15 miles out. Its two occupants were sunburned, thirsty, and half starved. They had sailed into the Bay from Boston and when they lost sight of land due to a thick haze, they lost all sense of direction.

After making sure they were all right, I asked what had been the problem. They said the compass didn't work; somehow it wasn't reading correctly. My mate and I inspected the instrument and found it was one of the most expensive models available — and it was in perfect working order.

After questioning the two men further, we found both to be high-level professionals in their respective fields.

My mate summed it up with a few words that I felt should be etched in stone. "You know, Capt.," he said, looking back at the boat we had in tow, "you don't have to be dumb to be stupid."

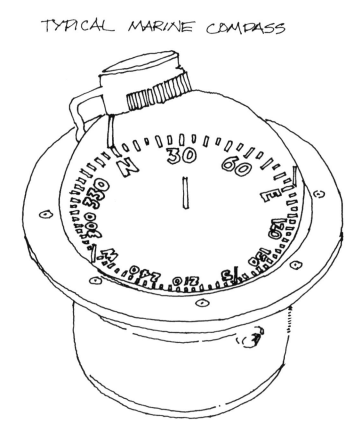

TYPICAL MARINE COMPASS

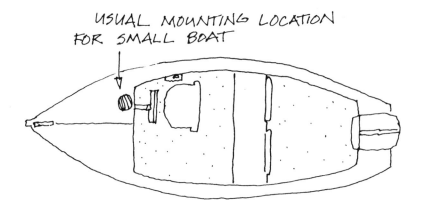

USUAL MOUNTING LOCATION
FOR SMALL BOAT

Other types of compasses that are in use today are electric-driven, gyro-operated, and are used primarily on large ships. Their cost would stagger your imagination.

All commercial aircraft and most private planes also carry *gyrocompasses*. The cost of these compasses isn't quite as high as the large ships' instruments, but the amount would still go a long way toward paying a family's annual food bill.

In most cases in which these instruments are used on ships or airplanes, a simple, inexpensive magnetic compass is used as a backup.

TYPICAL AIRCRAFT COMPASS

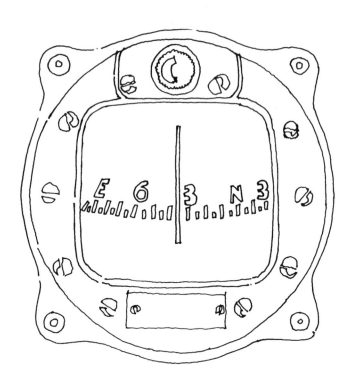

USUAL MOUNTING LOCATION
FOR AIRPLANE

SHIPS MAGNETIC COMPASS

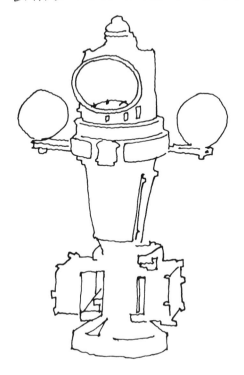

SHIPS GYRO COMPASS

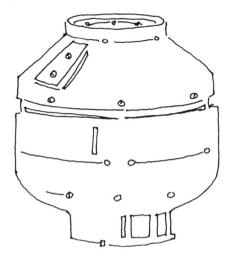

# CHAPTER 3

# COMPASS VARIATION

Well, now you've done it. You went out and bought yourself a shiny new compass, or maybe you borrowed one from that nice Scout next door. But, hold on a minute! Before you head off for the Klondike or begin your search for the lost treasures of El Dorado, there are still a few more details you should know about.

First of all, there's *compass variation*. Remember how earlier I said that a magnetic compass points towards a magnetic deposit? Well, that's true, but the *magnetic North Pole* is not in the same place as the true North Pole, as you will see in the following illustration.

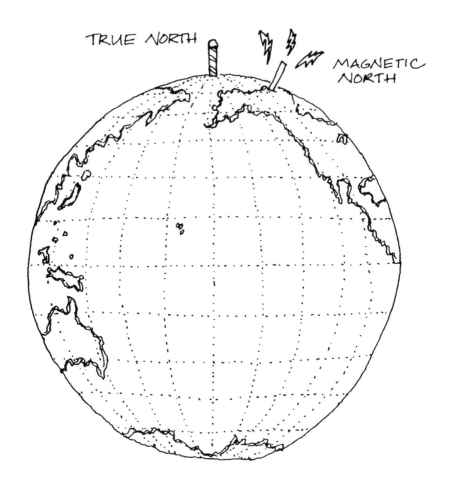

The Earth's magnetic field moves in somewhat erratic lines (called *Isogonic lines*) across the surface of the globe. Very few of these isogonic lines actually point true north.

For you to determine what the compass variation is in your area, you may want to purchase a U.S. Geological *survey map*, a *coastal chart*, or an *aviation map* for this information, or see the next illustration for an approximate idea.

Compass variation can be either east or west of true north. For example: let's say you are a New Englander and you have a 15-degree westerly variation. That means if your compass needle is on zero degrees magnetic north, true north will read as 15-degrees magnetic.

If you live in central United States, you may not have a compass variation at all as magnetic north and true north are likely to be the same for you.

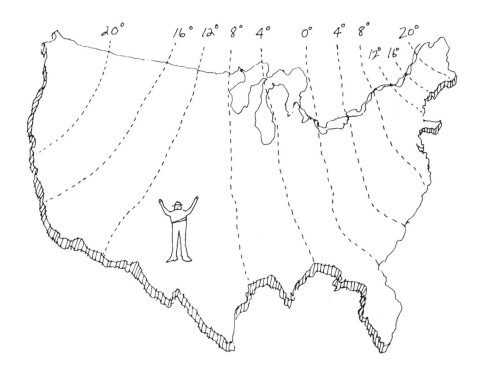

Those of you living in the western states will have an easterly variation. For example: If there is a 20-degree easterly variation in your area and the compass is aligned to magnetic north, then true north is 340-degrees magnetic.

The old rule is *east is least, west is best.* To put it simply, when converting from magnetic north to true north, add for west variations, subtract for east variations.

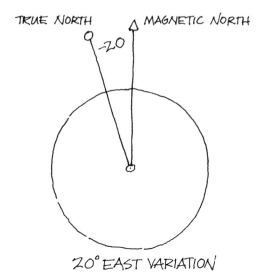

20° EAST VARIATION

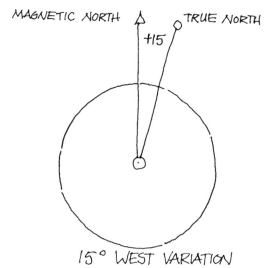

15° WEST VARIATION

EAST VARIATION
SUBTRACT
FROM
TRUE

WESTERN U.S.
HAS
EASTERLY
VARIATIONS

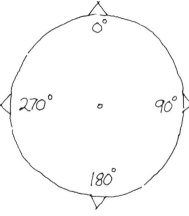

EASTERN U.S.
HAS
WESTERLY
VARIATIONS

WEST VARIATION
ADD
TO
TRUE

# COMPASS VARIATION EXERCISES

1.  You're walking 45° magnetic. What is your true heading if you have a 10° west variation?

2.  At 320° true with a 15° east variation, what is your magnetic course?

3.  At 20° east variation, what is the true heading of a magnetic course of 135°?

4.  At 12° west variation, what direction would you be going if you were walking 348° magnetic?

## Answers

1.  55°

2.  305°

3.  115°

4.  True north

You must remember that variation is the angle between magnetic and true north, and that variation changes with location.

At this point, let me remind you that in simple navigation there is little need to convert to true readings. However, a basic knowledge of true readings is necessary, as you will see in later chapters when we begin to work with the topographical map.

There are other factors that can affect the magnetic compass, and the most important is *compass error*. To see this factor at play, place your new compass on a table in front of you. Let the needle settle and turn the compass to align with magnetic north. Now, go get a hammer or screwdriver, or something else made of cast iron or steel. Move it around your compass and watch what happens to the needle. Notice how it moves toward the metal object you're holding.

This action doesn't mean your compass is defective. It just shows you that a compass can be attracted to other forces as well as to the Earth's magnetic field. An electric current from a nearby wire will drive that little needle crazy.

If you ever have to install a compass in your car, boat, snowmobile, or any other vehicles, you will undoubtedly have to correct the compass. Try to mount it as far away as possible from steel and sources of electricity.

Most compass manufacturers supply instructions and diagrams for how to correct the compass. However, the most important factor to remember is to make sure that the vehicle is pointing in a north-south direction before you adjust the instrument. You can do this by using your hand-held compass, but make sure you are away from the vehicle when you take the reading.

Once I had to install a compass in my pickup truck. I drove out to an empty supermarket parking lot with my two children one Sunday. I took a reading and had the children place plastic garbage pails at north and south headings. I then lined up the truck exactly between the two pails and adjusted the compass. It was when we were doing the east-west adjustments that the police showed up! I had a little explaining to do when my daughter informed the officer that he had to move his car because he was creating *magnetic interference* for her father.

When making adjustments on a mounted compass, you must always remember to use a brass or bronze screwdriver. If you don't have one, you can make one by filing down the end of a piece of brass welding rod.

While we're on the subject of compass interference, I'll tell you a story about a certain friend of mine who is a third-generation lobster fisherman with over four years of experience at sea. It was during our "monsoon" season, when weather systems pass over the Cape on an almost hourly basis.

What had been a sparkling blue morning quickly turned into rain and black fog. My friend had taken a sighting on a string of his lobster pots when the thick fog rolled in. Normally, there'd have been nothing to worry about; he had the compass course memorized and it would be just a couple of minutes until he would be in his pot line. Well, the couple of minutes turned into five, and the five into 10. My friend turned his vessel around and supposedly retraced his path for 15 minutes — still no pot lines.

At this point, he was in the process of inventing a new language when he discovered that a well-meaning relative had left a galvanized bucket full of 8-penny nails and a hammer aboard the boat. They had been repairing a beach house on a nearby peninsula and had forgotten to take the bucket when they left the boat. This in and of itself was not bad, but my friend's relative had placed the bucket on a shelf inside the cabin about 10 inches away from the bottom of the compass housing.

As he told me the story later on, he figured that if he had stayed on the course set by the bucket-induced compass error, he would have reached Iceland within six days.

There are plenty of other factors that can influence the magnetic compass but these occur mostly in aircraft-mounted instruments and in situations in which high speeds are involved. I feel that the explanation of these potential errors is not needed in this book, as they are not crucial to understanding simple navigation. However, for those of you who want to learn more on the subject, a list of excellent books will be given at the end of this volume.

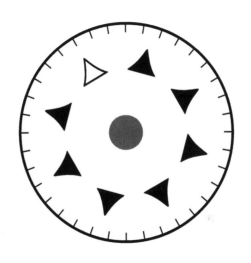

# CHAPTER 4
# LET'S NAVIGATE

This chapter will teach you how to use the compass while in the field, so before you set out, make sure you have a pencil, a small pad or notebook, and a watch. A comfortable pair of walking shoes will come in handy, too.

"But, I live in the city," you may say. Don't worry, you'll have just as much fun as your country cousin. Besides, when someone asks you what you're doing, you can impress the hell out of him by sticking out your chin and pointing along your direction of travel and exclaiming that you're following a magnetic bearing of such and such degrees. Just imagine what he will think!

## EXERCISE NO. 1
### There and Back Again

At whatever starting point you choose, face a landmark or the direction in which you want to go. Now hold your compass firmly in the palm of your hand and let the needle settle. When it's steady, slowly rotate the case until north comes under the needle. Now, look at your objective and the direction of travel to it and read the degree on the compass card that's pointing to the objective. If you have a direction arrow, turn it to that degree. Let's say your heading is 45-degrees. Walk to that objective.

Easy isn't it? Just for practice, read your compass and turn your direction arrow to the return heading 225 degrees (following our example of the original 45-degree heading) and go back to your starting point, only this time look at your watch and time yourself.

Let's say it took you five minutes to return, walking at the same pace. You now know that to get from your staring point (Point A) to your objective (Point B), you will follow a direction of 45-degrees for five minutes. To return it's five minutes at 225-degrees.

Should a thick fog limit your vision, you would still be able to get to your destination by frequently checking your compass.

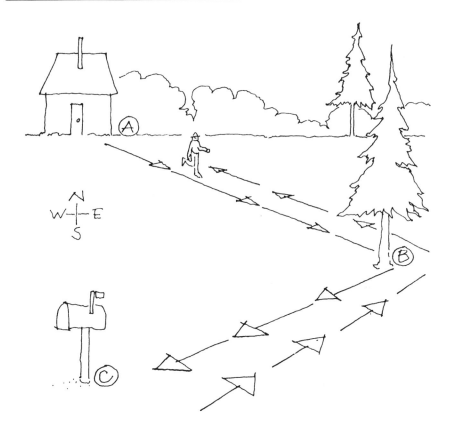

Using your own compass, indicate where magnetic north is on "A." Then, pencil in the degrees and name of directions by which you traveled.

Beginning at "A," what would be the degrees and directions that represent to and from "C?"

# EXERCISE NO. 2

## Around the Block or Backyard

This time, go around the block and write down each change of direction you make in your notebook, along with the time it took you to reach each point. You may want to draw a diagram for this exercise to help you understand the factor involved, or you can just fill in the blank spaces on the following illustration, after using your compass.

**A to B**

Direction _____

Degrees _____

Time _____

**B to C**

Direction _____

Degrees _____

Time _____

**C to D**

Direction _____

Degrees _____

Time _____

**D to A**

Direction _____

Degrees _____

Time _____

Did you have a nice walk? Now, write down the reverse headings of your trip, and draw a map of your walk. Perhaps it wasn't exactly square like the one in the diagram. At each direction change, draw a small circle and indicate magnetic north with an arrow. Then, as best as you can, give an approximate direction from B to D and A to C and their return headings.

Before going on to the next exercise, it might be a good idea to figure out how fast you move on average. An average person can walk a mile in 15 minutes, or 4 miles per hour. Those of you who jog will probably cut this time in half. If you are a hunter or are in the backwoods, your pace over broken ground will likely average about 2 miles an hour. Don't forget to take into consideration the type of terrain involved. Remember, you'll usually go downhill quite a bit faster than you'll go uphill.

Another thing you'll want to remember while you're practicing navigation is to take note of the position of the sun (if it's visible, of course). At each direction change, make a note as to the date and time of day and where the sun is relative to the direction in which you're walking.

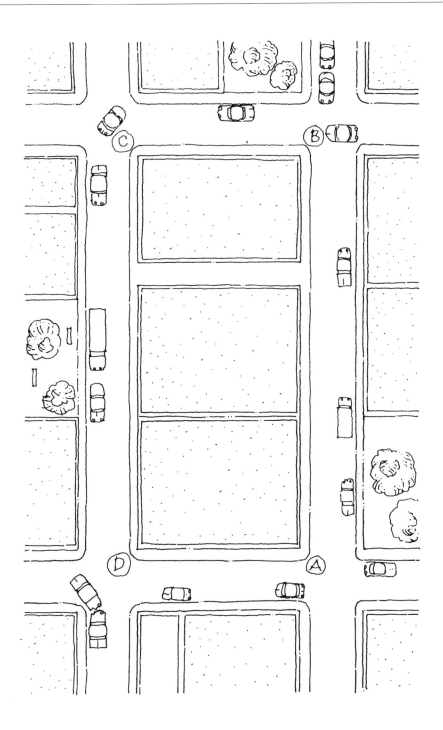

## A to B

Degrees of travel _____

Time to B _____

## B to C

Degrees of travel _____

Time to C _____

## C to D

Degrees of travel _____

Time to D _____

## D to A

Degrees of travel _____

Time to A _____

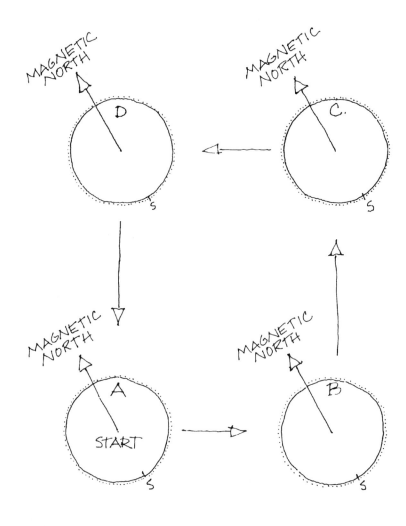

Noting the position of the sun serves two purposes. It will teach you how to judge a direction without a compass, and it will give you a guide mark while following a magnetic heading.

For example, if it's early in the morning and you're walking 90-degrees and the sun is directly in your face, you won't need a compass to know that you're walking east. By putting the rising sun on your right shoulder, you'll be facing north. Familiarity with this fact will come in handy should you lose your compass while in the field.

# EXERCISE NO. 3

## The Treasure Map

This exercise is meant for two or more people and can be a lot of fun for all involved.

First, you'll need something to bury or hide, like a six-pack of beer or a bottle of rum — something that everyone will enjoy when it is found.

Now starting from a given place, take a reading and time the distance between direction changes. The more detailed and intricate you make the map, the more fun everyone has, especially if they must crawl and climb over things to reach an objective. Instead of timing the distance between the last few direction changes, count the paces. Your friends will really love you if you find a nice swamp for them to wade through! Don't try to draw a map like the ones you've seen in pirate movies: just simply write down compass headings and time or paces.

EXAMPLE: Starting at the back door of Joe's Bar and Grill

95°     11 minutes

60°     9 minutes

260°    8 ½ minutes

20°     till you reach a stone wall

180°    3 ½ minutes till you reach a large oak, then 15 paces at . . .

140°    X marks the spot

You can double the fun by making another map with different readings, but both going to the same place. This means two or more teams can compete for the prize.

I'm sure you can be a little more imaginative in your map-making than I have been. However, don't forget to tell you friends that this type of exercise in navigation is not a black-tie affair. Cross-country skiers and snowmobilers can also play a form of this game, but everyone meets at the "X" for a cookout!

Write the compass headings and time your trip to the nearest grocery store. Use the space below to draw a map of your trip. Then as best as you can, determine what would have been the direct heading to your objective, providing that there were no obstacles in your way.

N

W                                                                    E

S

What general direction would you walk to return to base in the shortest possible time, or as the crow flies? Assuming you have followed a compass heading of 10° for 20 minutes, then changed direction to 70° for an additional 20 minutes? Use the space below to draw a diagram of this problem.

N

W                                                                                              E

S

# EXERCISE NO. 4
## Navigation Away from Civilization

This exercise is for people who spend time in the mountains, forest, or open country, and make a habit of venturing into unfamiliar places. Apart from the occasional weekend boater, hunters, weekend explorers, and cross-country skiers are more apt to get lost than any other group. We'll cover the particular problems of the weekend boater in a later chapter.

By now, you should be adept at using your compass and taking a reading. As you have seen, it's a very reliable instrument, as long as you know how to use it correctly. During this exercise, I hope to teach you to always trust it.

There have been times in my life when I could have sworn the darn thing was lying or not operating properly. I have been positive I was going in the right direction and the compass was very insistent that I was wrong. In all of these disagreements, the compass won.

I know of no hunter or outdoorsman who hasn't doubted his compass at one time or another. So when it happens to you, don't feel lonesome; others have been there before you. Always make sure there is nothing to influence the compass while you're taking a reading.

If you're hunting, lean your rifle against a tree and step away a pace or so. That nine pounds of steel held too close to your magnetized compass can send you off to rediscover North America if you're not careful while taking your readings. Another good idea is to tie the compass to your belt, so you won't lose it. I use a 15-inch piece of rawhide with a large loop in one end to slip around my belt. That way if my compass should fall out of my pocket, it won't go anywhere.

A close friend of mine, a man I've hunted deer with since I was a boy, tells the story of having lost his compass while hunting in a wilderness area of northern Vermont. It was snowing at the time and there were no familiar landmarks. As he said, everything looked the same. He sat down to reason the situation out when he discovered the compass had fallen through an inside hole of his pocket and down into his hunting pants, which, luckily, were tucked into his boots. He was wearing long johns and couldn't feel the compass against his leg as he walked. He got lucky and found his compass, but you may not be as lucky.

Now, let's get back to our exercise. First, find an area with roads you're familiar with; my best recommendation is a backcountry dirt road with woods on both sides. Park your vehicle and get well enough away from it before trying to read your compass (remember that metal can mess with your magnets!). Find out which way the road travels and jot it down in your notebook, drawing a line to represent the road. Next, choose a direction on either side of the road and find its opposite reading. For instance, let's say the road you're on runs north and south, and you plan to explore the west side of it. Make sure you make a note that you're heading into the woods on the west of the road at 270° and heading out of the woods east at 90°. Don't forget to jot that down, or your friends may never see you again! Your notebook information should look like this.

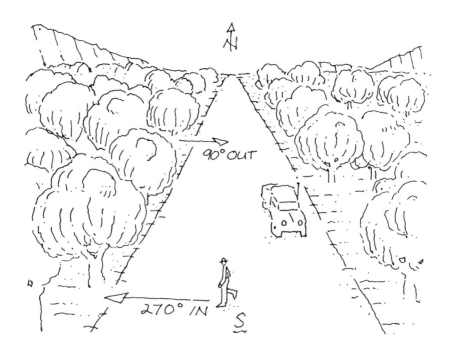

Use this space for drawing your own map.

N

W                                                                                    E

S

Now you know that no matter how far west of the road you go, you won't be lost. When it comes time to head back, all you'll have to do is walk east and you'll come out somewhere on the road on which your car is parked.

In order to give yourself confidence while you're in the field, put your compass away and spend a few minutes getting lost. Wander around a little and don't worry about the situation. It's kind of nice being away from the world for a while and letting go. When you're ready to rejoin civilization, the compass will guide you back.

The illustration on the next page will help you better understand this exercise.

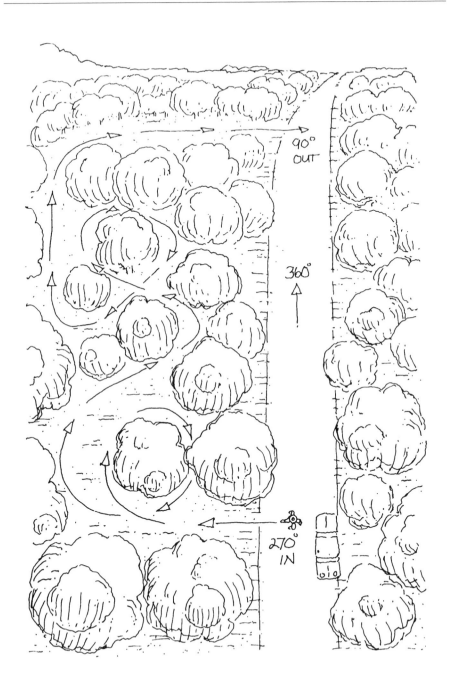

**1.** You are at X and plan to explore the right-hand side of this road. In what general direction would you be walking and what would your return direction be?

**A:** SW; E

**2.** You are at X and plan to walk in a northerly direction into the forest. What direction could you take to get back to the road other than south? Let's assume it's 4:00 p.m and you followed this direction. Where would the sun be in relation to your line of travel?

**A:** west; facing you

3. Let's assume you've lost your compass and you're at X. It's 10:00 am on a clear morning. What general direction would you walk to get back to the road? What would be the most direct direction towards your car?

A: west; northwest

If you noticed, in this exercise we made no mention of keeping time. This is because, for the most part, there was no need to do so. The important thing is that we learn to trust the compass and plan our direction before we started out. Most hikers and hunters I know track time in a general sense only. They estimate how long they have walked and how long it will take to get back. Time yourself on your first few trips into the field, but knowing in which direction to travel is most important.

There is one rule you definitely want to remember when in an unfamiliar area: *Always know where you are at least two hours before sundown.*

# EXERCISE NO. 5

## Estimating a Direction

This exercise is similar to the preceding one, only this time instead of wandering around, take a heading and parallel the road you're parked on — let's say 15-20 minutes of walking. Now, instead of taking your return heading out to the road, try to estimate what direction will take you out nearest to your car.

You just might surprise yourself and hit it right on the nose. And, if not, I'll bet you come close. You will probably also find that this exercise will teach you to save time by using the shortest distance. Another point to remember, as you grow more confident in wandering with a compass: always choose a reference point that you can't miss. A long road, a river, or stream, or a large, open field will work excellently as reference points. Never choose anything too small or indistinct, or you might walk past it.

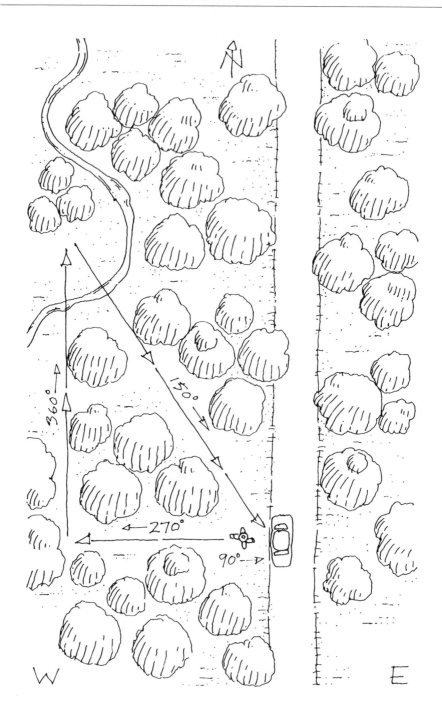

1. You're at X and have been following a compass heading of approximately 310° from the bridge. What would be the most direct heading to your car once you have returned to the bridge?

2. After walking a heading of 25° for one hour, you changed your direction to 130° and walked for an additional hour. What general direction would you walk to return to your starting place?

3. Return to start the shortest way, assuming you traveled on a heading of 215°, 300°, and 40° for equal amounts of time. Use the space below to draw a map of your journey.

## ANSWERS

1. 250°

2. west

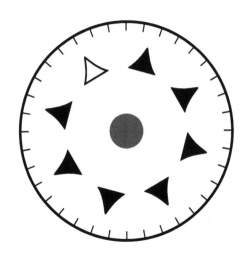

# CHAPTER 5

# CROSS-COUNTRY NAVIGATION

Cross-country navigation is the most advanced form of simple navigation that you can undertake. Above all, you'll need careful planning, confidence in yourself, and understanding of the use of some other tools besides your compass. The preceding exercises have taught you the basic principles of simple navigation using your compass. In cross-country work, you put them all to use while traveling over distances through wilderness or in completely unfamiliar surroundings to reach your objective.

Other than common sense and a good compass, the third most useful navigation aid you can to have at your disposal is a U.S. Geological Survey map of the area to which you're going. These maps can be purchased in sporting goods stores and bookstores, or you can download them for free from the U.S. Geological Survey's website, **www.usgs.gov**.

These Geological Survey maps are generally known as *topographical maps*, or topo maps for short, each of which covers the area of about a seven-mile square. Whichever term you choose to use will be correct. Should you decide to download the map from the internet, be sure to also download explanations for the chart symbols used on the map. We will cover the most important ones in this text, but there are many others worth exploring and understanding.

If you have never seen one of these maps, at first glance you'll likely find it interesting and almost frightening. All those thousands of little lines running all over the place; why, it's enough to make a grown may cry, you might say. Those lines are called contour lines and they have a story to tell. Suppose you are in an aircraft over mountainous country, and you are looking straight down. What would you see? At first glance, the country would seem flat or nearly so. It's only when you look at those mountains from above at an angle that you can get an idea of their shape and size.

Mapmakers, or cartographers, use contour lines to show us the shape of the land, while giving us a vertical view of it. Unless otherwise stated on your map, contour lines are shown at 20-foot intervals. The closer the lines come together, the steeper the grade. The following illustration will show you what I mean.

Looking a little closer at the contour lines, you'll notice that every fifth line is printed a little heavier and darker than its neighbors. These are the 100-foot intervals and are quite helpful for measuring short distances. If you see those 100 lines close together, you can bet that piece of ground is fairly steep! On the other hand, flat terrain with little change in elevation will be practically devoid of contour lines at all.

The height of most prominent hills or mountains on your course will be given in feet above sea level and will be printed near the summit on the map. If the elevation of a particular mound or hill isn't given, it's a simple enough matter to just count contour lines and multiply by 20 for your answer.

When looking at a topographical map, it's important to remember that not every flat surface has an elevation of zero feet. Suppose you're in the field and you're looking at a hill with a given elevation of 1000 feet and it appears to you to be only half that height. Remember that the plain or flat ground that you're standing on may be 500 feet above sea level and the hill starts on that plane. What you have is a 500-foot hill setting on a flat plain that's already 500 feet above sea level, zero feet.

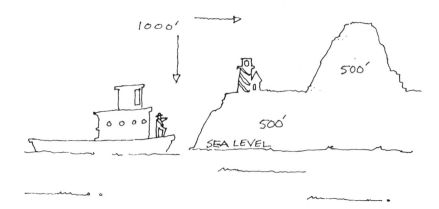

Geological survey maps are extremely accurate as far as positioning, contour, and elevation are concerned, and credit should be given to those geologists, surveyors, and pilots who developed them. However, for roads, highways, and trails, it's another matter. It's not that the ones marked on the map are in the wrong place, but rather, most geological survey maps were made in the late 1920s and our country and its network of highways, roads, and trails have gone through a lot of changes since then, while the landscape and mountains surveyed have not.

In other words, never attempt to use a survey map as a road map because a survey map is a picture of the land as it appeared to the mapmakers in the 1920s. Elevation and slope probably won't have changed much in that time, but everything else will have changed a great deal.

At the bottom of a survey map you'll find a set of scales, one in miles, another in kilometers, and another in feet. Using a straightedge, you can measure the distance between two points quite accurately. I am a little old-fashioned and still prefer miles to kilometers, but you can use whatever unit of measurement you find most convenient.

At the bottom of your map you will also find two arrows. One points toward true north, the other to magnetic north, and between them is the degree of variation from magnetic to true for the area covered by that map.

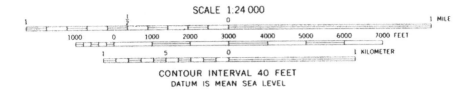

SCALE 1:24 000

CONTOUR INTERVAL 40 FEET
DATUM IS MEAN SEA LEVEL

THIS MAP COMPLIES WITH NATIONAL MAP ACCURACY STANDARDS
FOR SALE BY U. S. GEOLOGICAL SURVEY, WASHINGTON, D. C. 20242
A FOLDER DESCRIBING TOPOGRAPHIC MAPS AND SYMBOLS IS AVAILABLE ON REQUEST

UTM GRID AND 1967 MAGNETIC NORTH
DECLINATION AT CENTER OF SHEET

In the field, always make sure the survey map points to true north. To do this, first find the magnetic north; then use the direction arrow to indicate the true north heading. Now, set the map down facing true north. In case you haven't already noticed, the map has lines of longitude and latitude. Longitudes run north and south, while latitudes run east and west. Let's assume you're about to set out on a cross-country trip from a point that you have located on you map. Hold your compass directly over the map and turn the map until the longitude lines are pointing in the same direction as the direction arrow on your compass pointing to true north. When the map is lined up, step back and look around. Usually, about this time, you really begin to appreciate the work and precision that went into making these maps so long ago.

## UNDERSTANDING DEAD RECKONING

Of all the terms used in navigation, *dead reckoning* is the least understood, yet probably the easiest to explain. In a movie about Charles Lindbergh's epic solo flight across the Atlantic, Jimmy Stewart says the only thing wrong with dead reckoning is the word 'dead.' I agree. This term somehow evolved from the term *deduced reckoning*, which came from an era in which ships were made of wood and the men who sailed in them were supposedly made of iron.

Dead reckoning is a method of approximating your position by knowing how much ground you covered in a certain amount of time from a known starting position. Remember in an earlier exercise, I asked you to time yourself and find out approximately how fast you travel over different types of terrain. That information is the basis for determining a dead reckoning position. By knowing how fast you generally travel and how long you have traveled, you can estimate how far you have traveled from a specific location. Should you following a compass course outline on your survey map, you will be able to determine your position.

For example, let's say you left Joe's Bar and Grill at noon and you are traveling two miles per hour on a compass course of 270-degrees. The terrain is flat forest country, and you have very few landmarks to help you find your position. At the end of two hours, you want to see approximately where you are on the map. You know that after two hours you have traveled four miles.

Take a straightedge and measure the mileage scale at the bottom of the map; then place it along your direction of travel from Joe's Bar and Grill. Pencil in an "X" at four miles, as that's your dead reckoning position. As long as you haven't deviated from course and have taken into consideration any time you've spent resting, you will have a fairly accurate idea of your current position, and you will be able to estimate your time of arrival at your objective.

Always remember this: a dead reckoning position is an *estimated* position. Nothing takes the place of physical, recognizable landmarks on your map, and they, above all else, should be used as checkpoints when possible.

The term 'dead reckoning,' when used in reference to navigation at sea, is a method of estimating a ship's location between positions that, in most cases, are out of sight of land and have been determined by use of celestial navigation instruments. The methods and equipment used for dead reckoning on the sea are a bit more sophisticated, but the basic principles are the same.

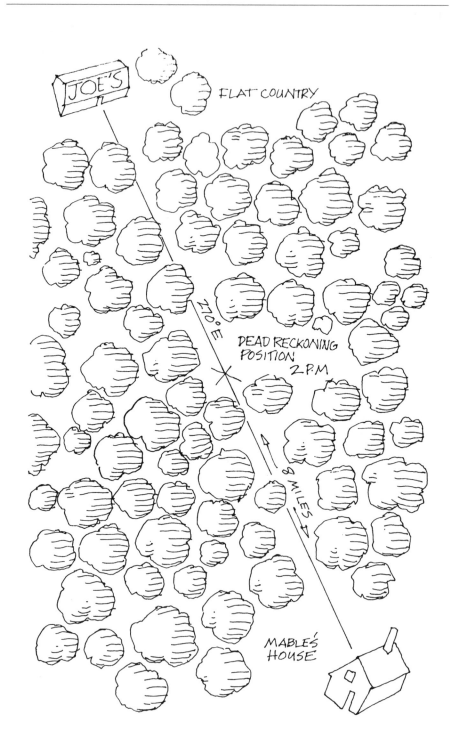

1. At a walking speed of two miles per hour through broken forest, indicate your dead reckoning position on the following map, assuming you had taken a course of 290-degrees and traveled it for an hour and a half.

   After having arrived at this position, what direction and how long would it take you to get to the lake?

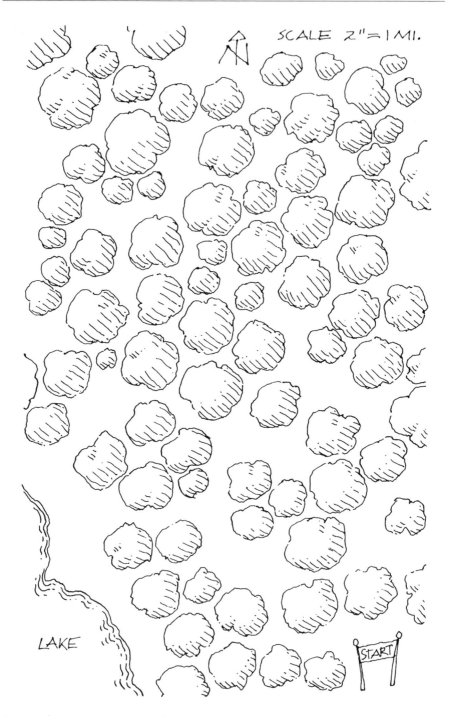

**A:** southwest; approximately 45 minutes

2. You are at X and your average traveling speed is two miles per hour. What direction should you take and how long will it take you to get to Joe's Bar and Grill?

   After leaving Joe's on a heading of 65-degrees and after having already traveled for one hour, indicate the remaining amount of time and what general direction to take if you want to go for a swim at the lake.

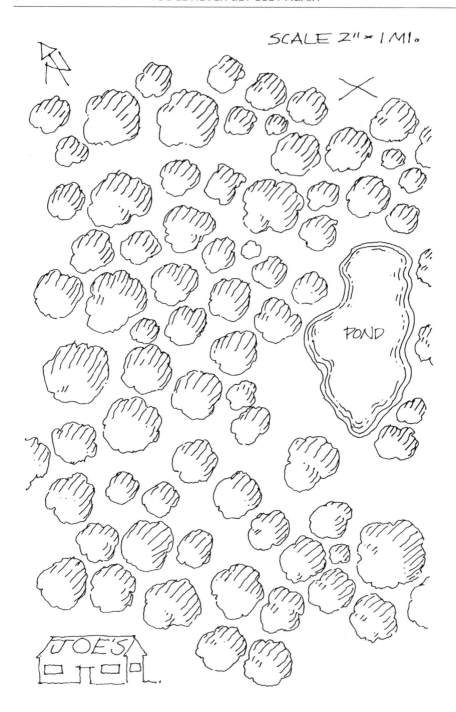

**A.** 250° for one hour and 45 minutes; southeast for 45 minutes

# PLANNING THE CROSS-COUNTRY TRIP

One of the most enjoyable parts of any trip into the wilderness is the planning and preparation. A little care in the beginning can save you a lot of unnecessary trouble, time, and expense, and make your stay away from civilization a pleasant adventure.

First, carefully study the survey map and familiarize yourself with the area through which you're going to be traveling. This way, you will be able to do all your navigation plotting long before you begin your trip. To do this, you will need a small ruler, a very sharp pencil, your compass, and a comfortable place to work. Don't worry about magnetic interference, you will only be using your compass card at this point; for now, forget about the needle. However, you might want to buy a protractor, which is a clear plastic semicircle with 180-degrees marked off in raised numbers. You could also use a marine or aircraft plotter, but the mileage scale might not match those on your survey map.

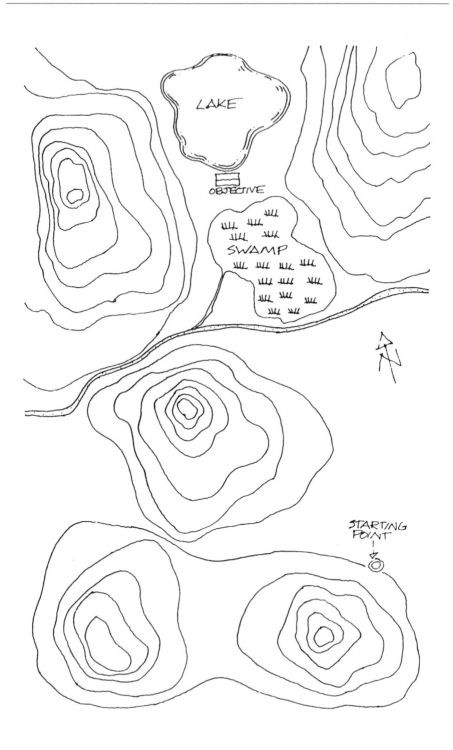

# PLOTTING YOUR COURSE

STEP 1        At your starting point, pencil in an "X" on your survey map. Then at each place you plan to visit, do the same, labeling them A, B, C, D, and so on.

STEP 2        Carefully look at the terrain between each stopping point and determine if you will be able to negotiate it. Why should you wade through a swamp when there might be a peasant little valley you could walk through instead? You might want to change your course a little.

STEP 3        Take your straightedge and pencil, and carefully draw a straight line between each stopping point.

STEP 4        Once again, look carefully at the terrain between each objective for suitable features that can be used as reference checkpoints. Mark each one with a check-mark.

STEP 5        This is the most difficult and important of your plotting, so pay close attention to your work. You must now find the true compass reading between each direction change on your course. If you have protractor or plotter, it's just a matter of placing the center hole of the instrument over the "X" or somewhere along the course line you've drawn. Then make sure it's lined up true north and south. When you've done this, read the degree your course line passes under.

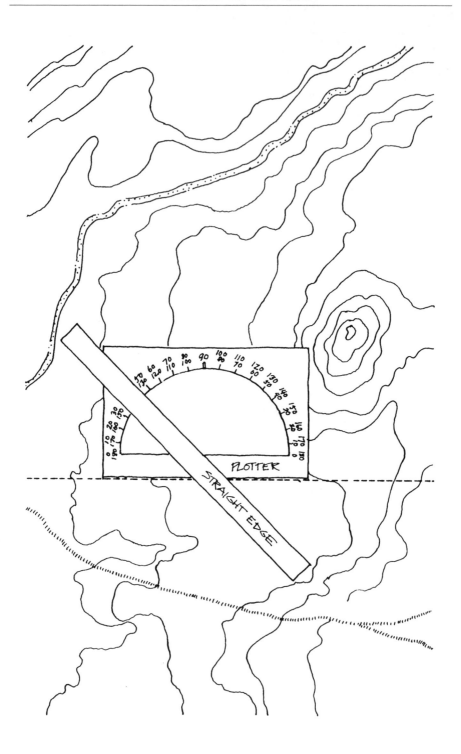

If you don't have a plotter or protractor, you can achieve almost the same results by using your compass, but you'll have to place the straightedge over the top or under your compass. Then, line it up precisely with your course line.

It's almost impossible to walk a straight compass course in a forest, or over rough, broken country, because you're continually dodging trees, boulders, washouts, and whatnots. Because of this, I advise you to pick prominent checkpoints. That way, if you're off a few degrees it won't matter. This point was driven home to me a long time ago when I first started to fly. I had planned a cross-country flight over the terrifying, forbidden jungles of central Massachusetts. One of the checkpoints I had chosen was a radio tower near a city of over half a million people. I was getting a little apprehensive because I couldn't find the thing when my flight instructor, Crash Mc-Loop, clouted me upside the head. He had a habit of doing this when I made even the slightest mistake. "You ingrate, you thankless earthworm!" he shouted into my already reddened ear. "You picked a needle for a checkpoint! Why the hell didn't you use the whole damned city?"

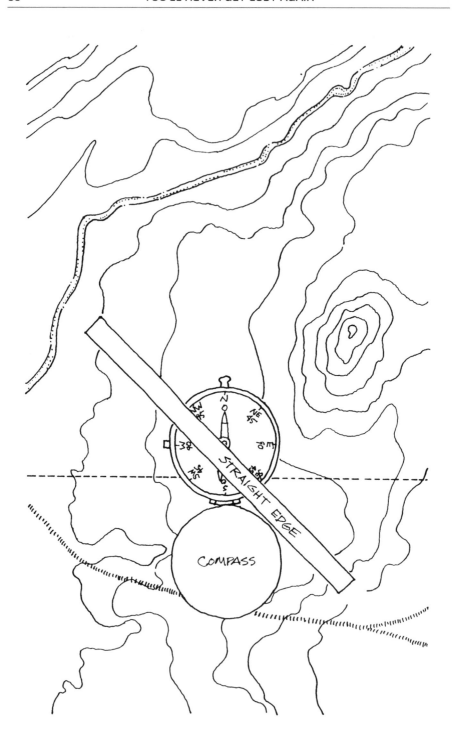

STEP 6    Convert the true course heading to magnetic. At the bottom of your survey map, you'll find the degree of variation. (See Chapter 4 if you need to brush up on how to use variations.) Now, pencil each magnetic heading and its reverse heading along the course line.

STEP 7    Using the scales at the bottom of your map and your straightedge, measure the real distance between each objective and checkpoint, and pencil it in along each course line. When you're finished, you can add up the total mileage of your trip.

STEP 8    Choose a direction from the area in which you'll be that will get you to civilization as quickly as possible in case of an emergency.

STEP 9    After plotting a course, always go over everything one more time to make sure you didn't make a mistake.

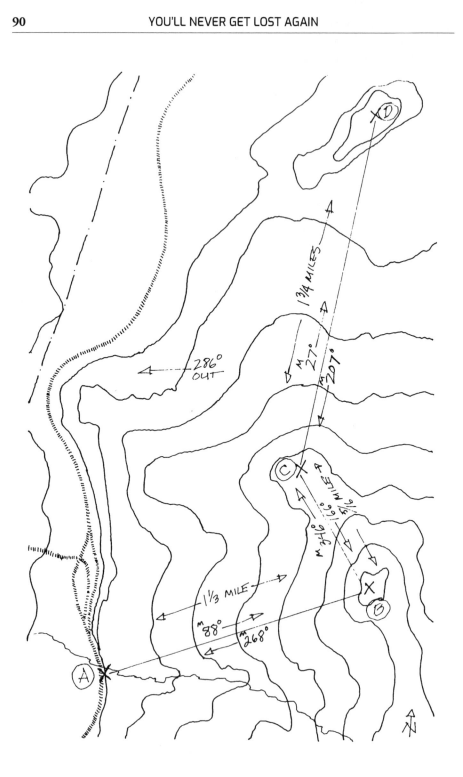

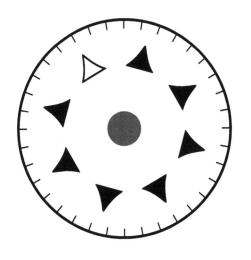

# CHAPTER 6

# SAFETY IN THE FIELD

## PREPARATION

Safety is the most important thing to consider in any planned venture away from civilization. Whenever possible, keep the odds in your favor.

Always let friends know where you're going to be and how long you'll be gone. Give them copies of your survey map with your navigation plot circled. They may not understand it, but a forest ranger or park warden will be able to use it to track you down should you need help or if there is an emergency. After considering the time factor and giving yourself plenty of leeway, say an extra day, you may give your friends a deadline and tell them to call the authorities if they haven't heard from you by that time. It's also always a good idea to stop by the nearest ranger or police station and tell them your plans. They may have information that could be helpful and save you some trouble. Perhaps the streams are swollen, or some big shot from the city has bought a tract of land and posted it.

Choose your equipment carefully. An overnight trip will not require a 50-pound pack. Always take into consideration the weather and the time of year when planning clothes. I personally prefer to travel light, as I find a heavy pack more of a burden and not worth some of the goodies it carries.

Make an equipment, clothing, and supplies checklist, and use it. On the following page is a starting list of items you may want to consider taking before leaving on a cross-country trip. In making up your own list, you should think twice about some of the things you pick. Is that battery-oper-ated, computerized, portable makeup kit and hair dryer really a necessity? You may also want to leave behind some of the extra food you were going to bring. Perhaps you could instead hunt for fresh game and gather edible plants that grow in the wild.

## EQUIPMENT LIST

- Spare compass (always a good idea), but don't forget to tie the first one to your belt.

- Extra map (for another member of your party).

- Large and small plastic bags (to keep things dry in wet weather). You can use the small ones for your navigation equipment and valuables, such as your wallet, notebook, and maps. Use the large ones (garbage bag size) for your pack and sleeping bag. Maybe you'll have to ford a stream or swim a river.

- Wooden, waterproof matches (you can make your own by melting some wax and dipping the tips in it).

- An 8-foot, square sheet of plastic. It weighs little and can be used for a spare tent or ground sheet, or even a large raincoat for everyone to get under in case of a downpour.

- Knives (I recommend a standard hunting knife with a 3- to 5-inch blade, and a small pocket knife or Swiss army clasp knife with all the extra doodads).

- If you wear eyeglasses, always take a spare pair along.

- A bright red or blaze orange hat or jacket if you're going to be in the forest during hunting season. We want you to come home behind the wheel and not across the fender.

- Your hunting license, if you plan to shoot game.

- A single shot 12-gauge shotgun with 20 rounds of assorted shot from number 7½ to a couple of rifle slugs. If you're going to be primarily exploring and traveling and only shoot to feed yourself and friends, this combination can't be beat. It's easy to carry, and with the variety of ammunition you can stop anything from a humming bird to Godzilla.

- 15 feet of ½-inch nylon rope. (This has a thousand uses, from holding up your tent to dragging out that big buck you just shot).

- Insect repellent.

- Snake bite kit, should you be in an area where the little beasties thrive.

- Portable, citizen band walkie-talkies for each member of your group.

- Obviously, you will want to consider such matters as flashlights, tents, sleeping bags, first-aid kits, and even extra food in case the hunting and fishing turn sour.

- Cell phone with portable charging battery.

- _____

- _____

- _____

*As you can see, there is an almost endless variety of useful things that you can take along, and you'll have to decide which of these are necessary for your own trip. But, remember this — someone has to carry it all.*

# LOST

Let's assume that you went and got yourself well and truly lost. Now you can throw up your hands to the heavens and issue forth that time-honored battle cry that rings like a clarion call across the length and breadth of our nation each summer and fall: "WHERE THE HELL AM I?" If you're in a group, there is a little variation of the call that's much too lewd to print here.

Well, now you've really got things to worry about. Let's say it's getting dark, the sky is overcast, and nothing looks familiar. Perhaps someday they will find the dust of your bones after the lions, tigers, bears, gorillas, and Big Foot get through with you, let alone the tree that stalks by night and the eggplant that ate Chicago. If none of these monsters bring about your end, there is one that will, and he can be the most dangerous enemy you will ever have in the wilderness if you don't keep him under control. That enemy is yourself. Your own imagination can do more damage than any animal you'll ever run into. (In most cases, when a wild animal gets your scent, it sets out to establish a new land speed record in the opposite direction.)

The first thing to do when you realize that you're lost is to admit it. Don't start walking fast or running; that won't solve the problem. Sit down and cool it for a few minutes. There are some important things to take into consideration. While you're sitting there regaining your composure, listen very carefully. Perhaps you can hear the sound of traffic on a distant highway or a farmer's barking dog or some man-made sound you can use to find your bearings. Remember, if you're in hill country, sound can seem to come from several different directions at once. Be sure you have the right one before setting out. Whether you can hear something or not, climb a tree or the nearest hill. From higher ground, maybe you will recognize a landmark or see where the sound is coming from.

Let's say you haven't heard or seen anything. Check your watch and estimate how much time you have before dark. You're going to need that time to find a nice comfortable spot to spend the night. If that sounds frightening, relax; you'll find your way in the morning. There's no big deal to spending the night in the woods.

Take the weather into consideration. Is it cold? Maybe it's started to snow. If so, you must keep as warm and dry as possible. I'm sure by now you have realized that the weather is a very real enemy in a situation like this. Try to find yourself a thick stand of pine or fir trees away from the wind, preferably on a gradual sloping hillside. This will help keep you dry and afford drainage should it rain. Now start gathering every stick of dry wood in sight and begin stockpiling it beside your campsite. If the wood on the ground is damp, use dead limbs from standing trees. One tip to remember should you be in an area where birch trees are available: birch bark will burn even if it's wet. You may want to gather some to help you start your fire. What if it's a warm, dry night? Build a fire anyway. It will give you something to do during the night, and if people are trying to locate you, the smoke and light will help.

In case you have lost your compass, find your westerly direction by getting a look at last light or sunset. You may have to climb a tree to do it, and when you have done so, draw a compass on the ground. You know by facing west, your right hand will be pointing north. Should you hear gunshots or sound signals during the night, you'll know what direction they came from and be able to follow them come morning. First light will give you your easterly direction.

If you've been hunting, wait until almost dark before trying to signal your friends using a gunshot. You wouldn't want to shoot too early in the day as they might think you were still just shooting at game. The standard rule is to fire three shots at well-spaced intervals, then listen. (Save one of your empty cartridges. It will make a wonderful whistle that can be heard from almost half a mile. Press the open end of the cartridge hard against your lower lip and blow). I personally don't recommend walking through a forest on a dark night. It's a good way to break a leg or fall into an empty well. Nevertheless, if the weather is clear and you can see the moon or stars, and the country you're in is not too rugged, go ahead. Just slow your pace and be extra careful. A little later on in this chapter, I'll show you how to find your direction by the stars.

Come the dawn's early light, you'll be ready to move. If you have a compass and a map, finding your position won't pose too much of a problem. First, get to high ground and line your map to true north. Then locate your last known position on your map and estimate approximately how much time you spent traveling from that position. I assume you already know how far you usually travel in a given span of time. For example, let's say you travel 2 miles an hour and you walked 2 hours before you realized you were lost. Now you know you are at least 4 miles from that last know position. By using the distance scale on your map, draw a 4-mile circle around your last position. Carefully study the lay of the land around you and see if any of it matches up with anything within the circle. If so, the rest is easy. Simply draw a line from your present position to one on your original course line. Measure the distance and pencil in checkpoints. Figure out the magnetic heading, estimate the time of travel, and off you go.

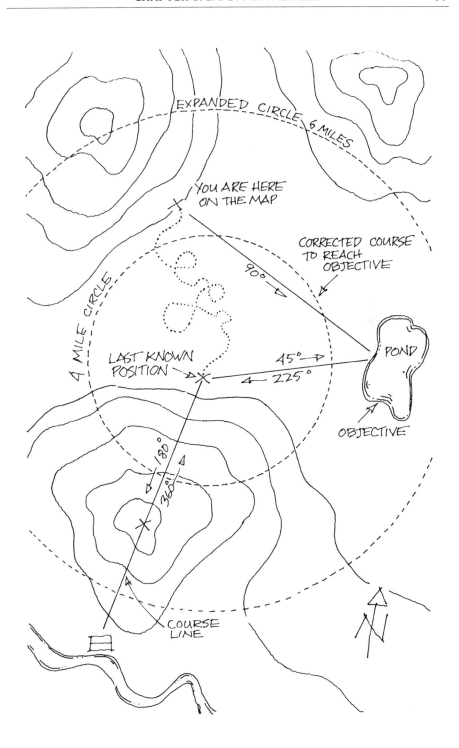

Now, let's suppose you are unable to locate yourself on the map. First, enlarge the circle by another hour and carefully look at the additional territory. No luck? Okay, climb to the top of the highest nearby elevation.

If by now you can't pinpoint yourself, you don't belong there. Remember, in the plotting phase of your trip you picked a direction to get you out of the wilderness some way, somehow. Well, now is the time to use it.

Let's go back a little. If you can't find your position, can you find water? Most streams, lakes, ponds, and rivers will be on the map, and you'll have at least a general position with which to work. If not, it will eventually lead you out, but I still recommend you stick to your pre-planned get-back-to-civilization direction. That stream may take you a long way before you get out.

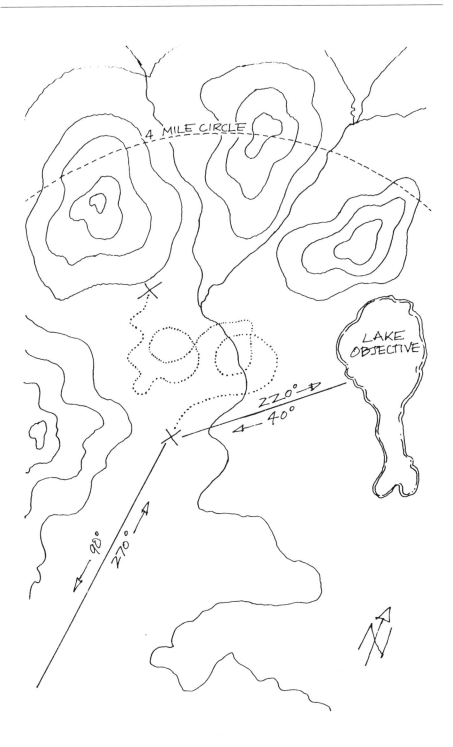

Just for a moment now, let's put the shoe on the other foot. Instead of being lost yourself, suppose you are searching for a friend. If you have an idea of where your lost friend is, and you have a vehicle that can get into the area, go as close as possible to where you think he is and blow your horn three-well-placed blasts every 2 minutes, and listen for a return signal. Another instrument you can use to attract attention just short of waking the dead is a chain saw. Nothing in this world makes a racket quite like this machine. During the day the sound is almost intolerable, and at night it's obscene. If you're within 10 square miles of the lost person, he will hear it. Just remember, he may be a long way off, so keep up a steady racket, which will enable him to home in on you.

Should you be at a campsite and a member of your party doesn't make it back before dark, make a big fire (being careful not to let it spread, of course), and then make a lot of noise. Gunshots, pots, pans, whistles, anything at all will be helpful. You may have to keep up this racket half the night, but most of the time it does the trick. Never leave a campsite to look for a lost friend at night. At best, you can only travel a few miles an hour on foot. Sound, on the other hand, travels at about 700 miles an hour. Besides, you could wind up getting lost or hurt yourself. If you haven't located the lost person within a reasonable amount of time — let's say between two to five hours — you should contact the authorities.

## GETTING OUT WITHOUT A COMPASS OR MAP

You have two choices here. If you're sure someone has started a search for you, or if you or someone with you is injured, your first choice is to stay where you are. Should this be the case, find a clearing and keep a fire going, a nice, big smoky one. If there is snow on the ground, stamp out a *huge* SOS. If you have a big enough clearing, make your sign immense. One about the size of a football field will do quite nicely. Then, line the letters with branches and leaves to make it stand out more from above. A fixed-wing aircraft at its slowest speed is traveling around a mile a minute, and it doesn't take long for one to fly right by you. The bigger your signal, the better chance you have of being spotted and rescued.

Your second choice is to move. Get going at first light. Maybe you don't have a compass or map, but the sun can be just as good. Try to remember the direction you planned to use to get you out of the wilderness in an emergency and use the sun as your guide. If the day is cloudy and overcast or it's snowing, without having something to give you a general direction, you'll just walk in a circle. My best recommendation is to keep heading for low ground until you eventually find water. No matter how small the stream, it will lead you to larger ones. If you should happen on a cart trail or grown-over logging road, remember that the vehicle that made them had to come from somewhere, so follow the trail. Should you come to a dead end, then it's at least certain that going the other way will take you out.

People are always telling me how you can find north by looking for moss and fungus that grows on the north side of trees. Well, that's technically true, but it also grows on the east, west, and south sides. Next time you're in the field check it out for yourself. Tree trunks that are always in the shade may have growth all around them. I would use this method of finding direction only as a last resort.

## TRAVELING AT NIGHT WITHOUT A COMPASS

As previously stated, you can get about at night without your compass, provided the weather is clear and the terrain you're on is not too rugged. There is one exception to this that can be quite helpful. Lights from towns, villages, and highways will reflect on a low overcast and can be seen for miles. You may be able to guide yourself based on these reflections until you find civilization or use them to establish a direction line that you can follow in the morning.

The other way is to do what man has done for centuries: follow the stars. As a charter boat captain, one of the things I enjoy most is taking anglers game fishing at night, especially if the sea is calm and there is no overcast. Once I am out of the harbor and clear of all obstacles, I point the bow toward a familiar star and do some fishing myself. My vessel, the *Sea Witch*, has all the best electronic navigation equipment aboard, but, when possible, I'll chase a star to my destination instead. This method may not sound scientific, but it sure puts a little romance back into running a boat.

The following illustration of the night sky will show you how to find the North Star at different times during the year. Once you've located it, you have found a fixed position directly over the North Pole. Throughout the night, the heavens appear to rotate around this star as the Earth revolves, the North Star never moving. You must remember this. Should you be guiding on a star near the horizon, keep checking your direction of travel by the North Star. You may want to change the star you're guiding on after a while as the stars shift in the sky. Another thing to remember is that the North Star isn't the biggest one in the sky. You'll have to do a little looking before you recognize it.

22

x

## Spring

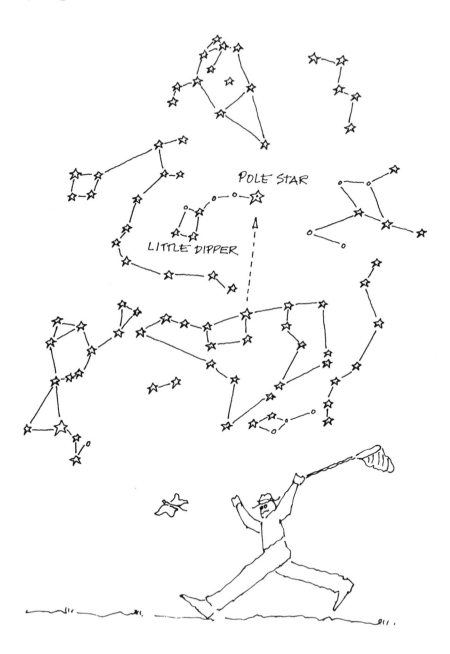

POLE STAR

LITTLE DIPPER

## Summer

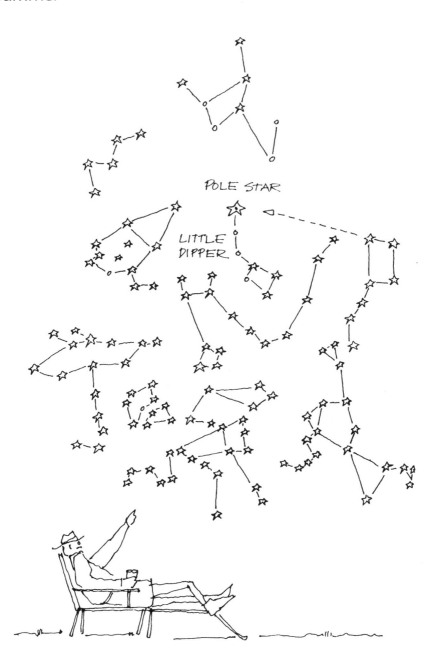

# Fall

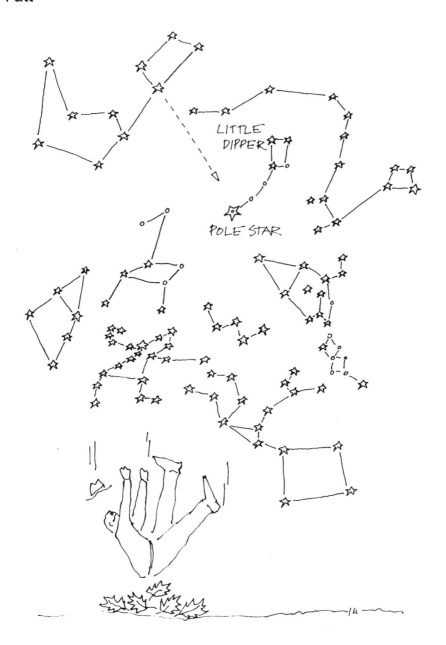

# Winter

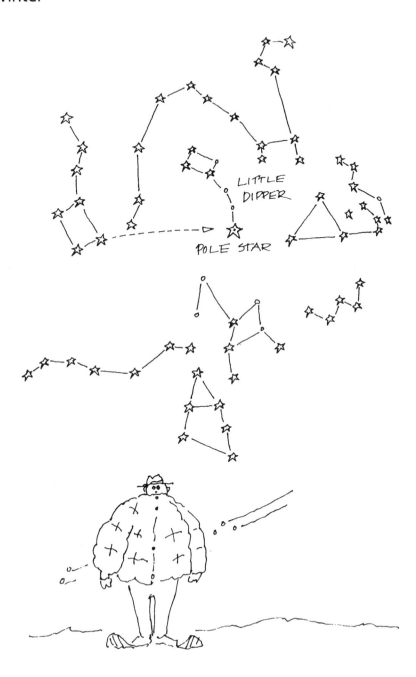

# CHAPTER 7
# NAVIGATION FOR THE BOATMAN

The subject of marine navigation is a detailed science with many facets. The purpose of the following chapter is only to acquaint you with a few fundamentals of piloting and is not to be considered a complete explanation by any means. However, the amateur boatman will find the information helpful for maintaining safe navigation of his vessel and as a foundation for more advanced navigation techniques.

Each year, tragically, history repeats itself along America's waterways, especially along the Atlantic coast. Hundreds of people set out in their boat and are never seen alive again. There are also many thousands who become lost or involved in marine-related accidents. After almost 40 years at sea, it is my personal belief that 75 percent of these accidents were inevitable. The key ingredients of accidents and tragedies like these are the words "neglect" and "forget," not to mention plain, old stupidity in its most basic form.

The story behind each fatality and mishap usually sounds something like this: "I neglected to learn how to use a compass;" "I forgot to fix the bilge pump;" "I didn't bother to check the weather;" "I didn't slow down in the fog;" "I didn't replace . . ." "I didn't check . . ." "I didn't think . . ." And then there is the greatest undoer of all time — the great stupidity: "I was drunk."

It never ceases to amaze me how people sometimes seem to go out of their way to get killed. The following story is a good example of this. Several years ago, in early spring, three men decided to make a trip from an upper

Cape harbor to Provincetown, a distance of nearly 30 miles. Their vessel was an 18-fool fiberglass runabout with a large 125-horsepower engine. The weather forecast called for a northeast storm with winds of 30 miles per hour, gusting to 50 mph. They had a full tank of fuel at six gallons. The storm had set in before they left, but do you think this stopped these "brave" souls from meeting their destiny? Of course not. Off they went into the teeth of a northeast storm in an 18-foot boat with 6 gallons of fuel. I know this is a little hard to believe, but it gets even worse. A trawler captain whose vessel was tied to the dock saw them loading up and tried to warn them, but he was rewarded for his efforts with what appeared to be a one-finger salute. Well, to make a long story short, one body was found and the other two were never seen again. The Coast Guard and the newspapers reported it as an accident — I suppose for lack of another word. I, however, have chosen a term that seems to fit this incident and several I know of like it: "Stupidcide." It was simple, unmeditated stupidcide. Their chance of survival was about the same as if they dressed in fuzzy, brown suits with antlers and ran through the woods during the opening day of deer season.

Safe boating is a combination of many factors:

1. Good equipment

2. Careful planning

3. Accurate information

4. Thorough inspection

5. Know the rules of the road

6. Know your vessel's limitations

7. Know your own limitations

8. Just plain common sense

Always keep the odds in your favor and your trip on the water will be rewarding and enjoyable.

One recommendation that I can make to the beginning boatman is to join a power squadron of your local Coast Guard auxiliary, or at least enroll in one of the many courses they offer. You'll learn a lot of useful things and have a lot of fun too.

## THE NAUTICAL CHART

Understanding the nautical chart will require a little effort on your part, but in comparison to a geological survey map, you'll find it delightfully easy to use. One of the first things you'll notice is that there are printed compass roses in convenient places around the chart. The outer circle gives you true heading and the inner one magnetic heading. Each rose is printed with the variation indication on its center.

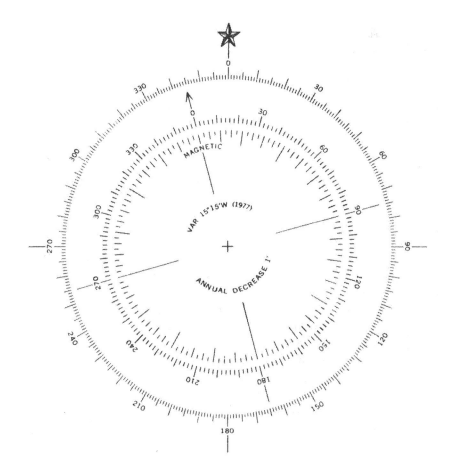

To plot a course, all you'll need is a straightedge and a pair of parallel rulers. Simply draw your course line on the chart. Now, place the outer edge of the parallel ruler along the course line and swing the other edge over the center of the nearest compass rose. You can now read the magnetic and the true heading. You won't have to worry about figuring the variation because the chart maker has done it for you.

## NAUTICAL CHART OF HARBOR

Nautical charts come in four different types, beginning with the *harbor chart*, which shows a detailed view of a small area. Every boatman should have one on his home port and familiarize himself with it.

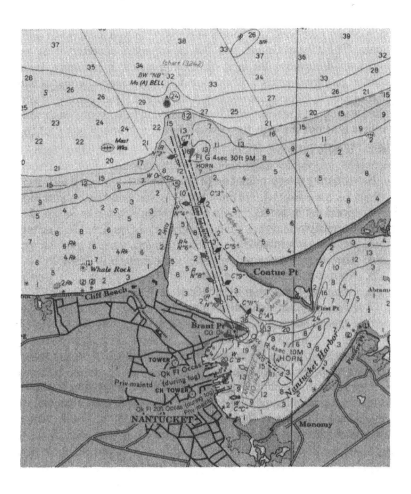

The second on the list is the *coastal chart*. This type of chart covers a somewhat larger area showing bays, harbor entrance sound, and all navigation aids. They are ideal for the beginning boatman, as they will enable him to navigate safely near the shore.

Next is the *general chart*, which is used primarily for coast-wide navigation, where a vessel may still be able to see shore but remain far enough away to avoid coastal dangers. Offshore fishermen and weekend yachtsmen find these charts ideal for their purpose.

Another chart, which is of little use to the average boatman, is the *sailing chart*. It covers a huge area and is used by ships to obtain their position before making shore. I use this type of chart aboard my aircraft when fish spotting. They are excellent for use in following the migrations of game fish.

Always check the scale on each chart you use because they tend to vary from chart to chart. Unlike survey maps, they are reprinted quite often, showing the latest changes and obstructions. It's a good idea always to keep them up to date.

Why are all the numbers scattered all over the place you ask? In a way, they are just like the contour lines on a survey map, but instead of showing you the lay of the land, they show you the depth of the water.

Check your chart, because sometimes the soundings are given in fathoms as well as feet. Just to save you from diving for your dictionary, a fathom is six feet. The depth shown on charts is given at normal low tide.

If you intend to operate in a coastal region, you will need a *tide table*. This will give you the times of high and low tide each day in a specific area. I advise you to check with your local marina or Coast Guard station about the tide factor before setting sail. Tidal currents in narrow places can be extremely dangerous, and knowing when and where they occur will help you to avoid them. Charts are available at most marinas and ship supply houses, or you can simply search on the internet and download them.

I suggest that you read all the information that's given before using your chart. It will only take a few minutes and there may be something you'll want to know before plotting your course. For example, some areas off-shore are used by the armed services for bombing and gunnery practice. Even a near miss will definitely spoil your day.

## AIDS TO NAVIGATION

Any person who drives a motor vehicle in the United States can get into it and drive to a city that is unfamiliar to him, over roads that he has never traveled before, just by following road signs. These are aids to navigation. The boatman does pretty much the same thing when he navigates in coastal waters. He uses a combination of man-made and natural landmarks to tell him where he is. On a highway, you may encounter signs that tell you there's danger ahead or to avoid a certain area.

On the water, you have the same tools. A lighthouse is one, for instance. Understanding and recognizing aids to navigation is of paramount importance to the boatman. On the following pages, you can see the basic buoy system of the United States. You should pay particular attention to the ones that apply to your area. One helpful exercise you can do after obtaining charts of your area is to match up as many symbols as you can with the following ones. In these illustrations, those buoys marked "port" are kept to the left, those marked "starboard" to the right, of the channel when heading *upstream* [or from a larger body of water to a smaller one elsewhere. Obviously, you must keep them on the other side when going the other way.

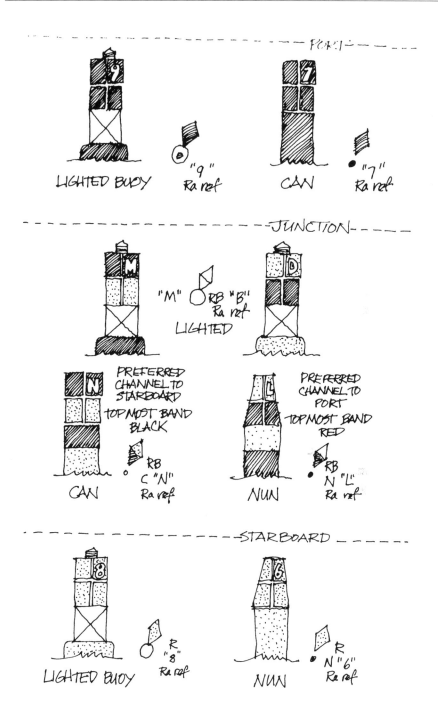

PORT

LIGHTED BUOY    "9" Ra ref

CAN    "7" Ra ref

JUNCTION

"M"  RB "B" Ra ref    LIGHTED

PREFERRED CHANNEL TO STARBOARD    TOPMOST BAND BLACK

CAN    RB C "N" Ra ref

PREFERRED CHANNEL TO PORT    TOPMOST BAND RED

NUN    RB N "L" Ra ref

STARBOARD

LIGHTED BUOY    R "8" Ra ref

NUN    R N "6" Ra ref

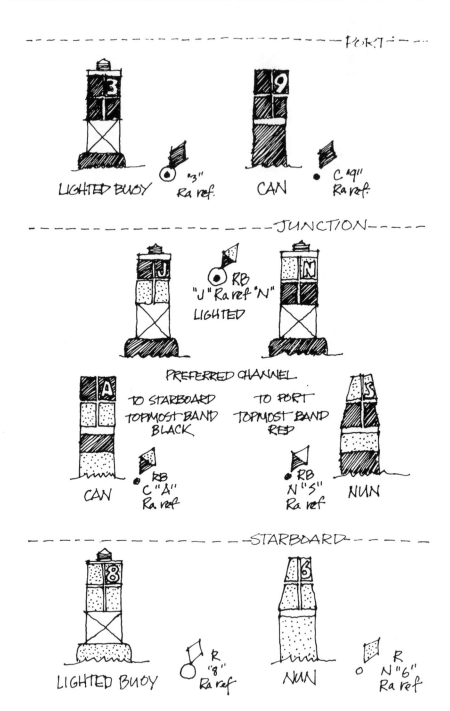

PORT

LIGHTED BUOY    "3" Ra ref.

CAN    C "9" Ra ref.

JUNCTION

"J" Ra ref "N"    RB
LIGHTED

PREFERRED CHANNEL

TO STARBOARD
TOPMOST BAND
BLACK

TO PORT
TOPMOST BAND
RED

CAN    RB C "A" Ra ref

RB N "S" Ra ref    NUN

STARBOARD

LIGHTED BUOY    R "8" Ra ref

NUN    R N "6" Ra ref

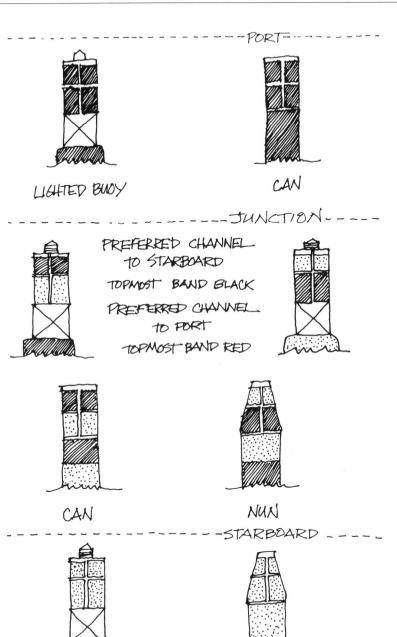

PORT

LIGHTED BUOY                          CAN

JUNCTION

PREFERRED CHANNEL
TO STARBOARD
TOPMOST BAND BLACK
PREFERRED CHANNEL
TO PORT
TOPMOST BAND RED

CAN                          NUN

STARBOARD

LIGHTED BUOY                          NUN

DIAMOND SHAPE WARNS
OF DANGER!

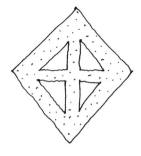

DIAMOND SHAPE WITH
CROSS MEANS BOATS
KEEP OUT!

CIRCLE MARKS A
CONTROLLED AREA.

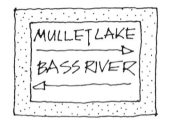

SQUARE OR RECTANGLE
GIVES INFORMATION,
NAMES, ACTIVITIES.

# PLOTTING ON THE NAUTICAL CHART — STEPS 1 THROUGH 5

Earlier we showed you how to plot a course on the survey map. If you're going to use a course you have plotted and followed on numerous occasions, after a while all the landmarks, and even the vegetation, along your way will become familiar to you;  eventually you won't need your chart or even your compass to follow it. As long as you can see, you'll be able to stay on your trail. The boatman, on the other hand, must be able to follow his trail even though his visibility may be limited to a few yards and there are no identification markers between each reference point.

When plotting your navigation courses for your area of operation, you must assume that one day you'll get caught in a low-visibility situation. Fog, heavy rain, and thick haze can easily be navigated in, provided you have done your homework and planned for their inconveniences beforehand.

Usually when I get to this subject during a discussion in the classroom, someone, and there always is one, sticks up his bony little hand and says, "So just use your radar." I answer this by telling him that we will pretend he left the cover off during maintenance and a sea gull dive-bombed it, and now, because of his negligence, the wretched thing won't work. At this point, every navigation tool in the book gets mentioned from other students from fathometers, radio direction finders, and loran sets to an occasional big ball of string. I tell them all that I conveniently put all those tools in the hockshop or left them on dock, and we're left only with the chart and the compass.

To make this information as clear as possible, let's assume that you're going to be operating your vessel from a small sheltered harbor that empties into a large body of water.

STEP 1          With a straightedge, draw your course line from your harbor to the harbor entrance buoy. See the following illustration.

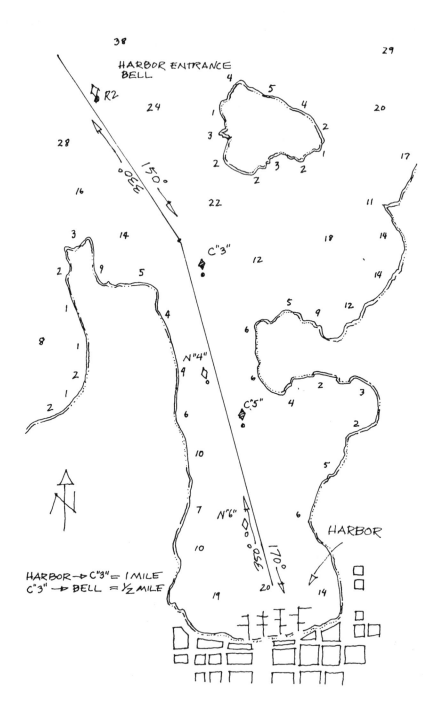

STEP 2    Now, using your parallel ruler as we showed you earlier, find your magnetic headings and write them down on your course line along with their reverse readings.

STEP 3    Next, carefully measure the distance between each buoy and write the information clearly under each course line.

STEP 4    At this point, the best way to obtain the rest of the information required is by getting it on the water. Choose a day when you have excellent visibility and you'll be able to sight one checkpoint from another. As you leave your harbor, set your throttle so you will be able to maintain a slow but steady operating speed. Remember, in low visibility you have to go slow to be safe. Check your tachometer or speedometer or both, and record this information on your chart or notebook. Then leave the throttle *alone*.

STEP 5    Time yourself between each buoy and record the time. Also, check your compass. You'll be pointing your bow right at these buoys as you make your run. If there's a small compass error, or the buoys are not quite in the same position in the water as they are on the chart, you will be able to see the differences and make the appropriate changes.

Remember, if you are in a coastal area where tide is a factor, you will want to record the stage of the tide, and the direction and speed of the current. If this is the case, when you reach the channel entrance buoy, turn your boat around and run the return course. This way you'll find the difference in time between checkpoints going with and against the current. It will vary at different states of the tide, but usually not enough to cause any great amount of trouble. You'll either get there quicker than expected or it may take you a little longer. The important thing is to stick to your compass.

Should you become encased in total fog and you miss your checkpoints, don't run aimlessly about and waste fuel. Drop your anchor, post a lookout, and blow your horn to warn other vessels and listen for their reply. You may be a little late getting back, but you'll get back.

The following illustration shows information compiled in notebook form for navigation in limited visibility.

### Marine Navigation Form

| Check Point | Mag. Course | | Distance | Time | Speed |
|---|---|---|---|---|---|
| | To | Return | | | |
| 1. HARBOR | C"1" | 350°/170° | 1 MILE | 15 MIN. | 4 KTS. |
| 2. C"1" | BELL | 330°/150° | ½ MILE | 7½ MIN. | 4 KTS. |
| 3. | | / | | | |
| 4. | | / | | | |
| 5. | | / | | | |
| 6. | | / | | | |
| 7. | | / | | | |
| 8. | | / | | | |
| 9. | | / | | | |
| 10. | | / | | | |

Tachometer Setting  11 RPM

Speedometer Reading  4 KTS.

E T A  12:00 P.M.

A T A  12:05 P.M.

Tide  HIGH

Current  ½ KT.

Notes:

Emergency Radio Channels  CH 9 CB
VHF CH 16

Weather Channel  162.55

# ELECTRONIC NAVIGATION AIDS

The rest of this chapter will be devoted to basic description and use of some of the pieces of equipment that we left at the pawnshop a few pages back.

## Depth Finders

Other than a good radio or a good first mate, a depth finder is one of the most valuable pieces of gear you can have aboard your craft. The machine works by transmitting an ultrasonic signal toward the bottom and measuring the time it takes for the signal to return. These machines come in two parts: the indicator, which is usually mounted near the helmsman (that's the boat driver), and the transducer, which is externally mounted on the bottom of the boat. Depth finders also come in portable units for use in small outboards and runabouts. The transduce, then, is usually attached to the stern or side of the vessel.

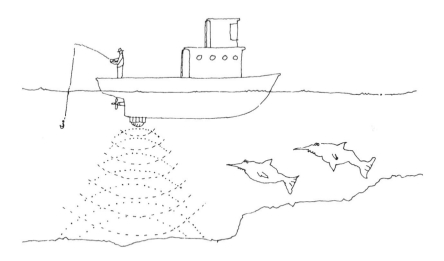

*Radio Direction Finder*

## Radio Direction Finder

This device gives you bearings to shore-based radio transmitters. The instrument consists of a radio receiver with several operating bands. A 360-degree circular grid is usually affixed to the top of the case with a tunable loop antenna in its middle. The use of the instrument requires a little practice and a lot of understanding of its principles of operation. The manufacturer usually supplies this information.

However, to explain the use of one of these sets as simply as possible without going into great detail, first choose a known shore station and turn your tunable antenna until you find the best reception. Then, turn the antenna away until you find its low or null point and read the degree on the grid on top of your set.

In order to use the RDF properly, you'll need to know where the radio transmitters are located on your chart.

R.D.F.

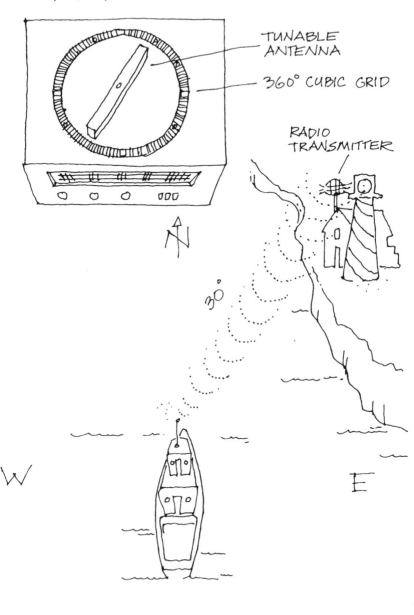

TUNABLE ANTENNA

360° CUBIC GRID

RADIO TRANSMITTER

N

30°

W

E

S

## Radar

The word means radio detection and ranging. To a vessel at sea in a thick fog, radar is one of the most useful pieces of equipment ever developed. Radar not only shows you objects around you, but it also tells you how far away they are. In navigation you can fix your position early by measuring the distance from known objects. Also, should the object be moving, you can determine its speed and direction of travel. A radar set operates by transmitting high frequency radio impulses or waves at a given rate. When these impulses strike a distant object, they return and create an outline of the object on the receiver.

The only drawback I can think of with radar navigation is that most people become overly reliant upon it and should the set malfunction, they can get into trouble. Also, radar sets are quite expensive and the amount of space they take up generally limits their use to vessels larger than 25 feet.

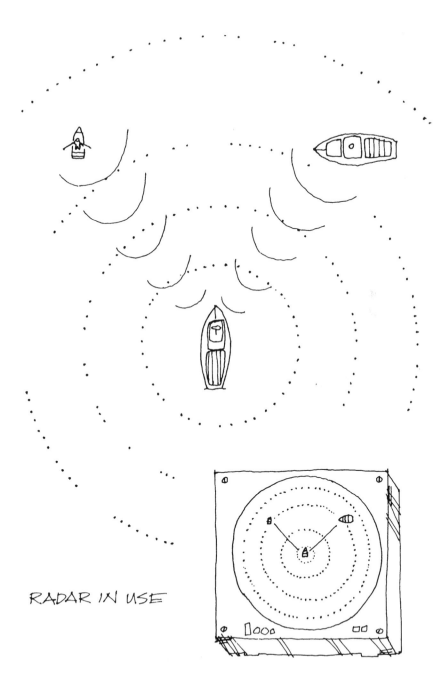

RADAR IN USE

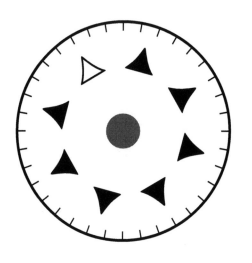

# CONCLUSION

Since the first edition of this book was originally published, I have received many letters from people from all walks of life, all over the globe. Most of these were positive and thanked me for simplifying what seemed to them to be a complicated science; many were about having been lost but being able to find their way back; others were about having planned trips to hike in the wilderness; some were downright funny. However, there was one letter that had nothing to do with navigation, but everything to do with the compass that led them to a monumental discovery in a far western state.

Three hunters were in the high country on a sheep hunt when they came across a stream that led to a small valley several hundred feet below them. The stream was flowing south down the side of this mountain range. In the letter, it said that they took a lunch break beside the stream when one fellow decided to check their position on a map. He took out his compass to take a reading, but when he looked at the needle, it was spinning wildly, reminiscent of a windmill.

"What is wrong with this thing? The needle is going nuts!" he said.

His two partners took out their compasses, only to find that theirs were spinning, as well.

'We did not know it at the time,' he wrote, 'but we were standing on one of the largest iron ore deposits in the west.' They are now very wealthy men.

I also received a letter from the dean of one of the most prestigious colleges in New England. He wrote to me about a certain fraternity that had given three pledges the check points and compass courses that led them, one at a time, from different starting points to a certain house in a nearby city. The pledges were to return with evidence of some proof that they had been there. Several returned with articles of feminine apparel, but two returned with a car full of young ladies that were employed at the premises. It never said in the letter, but I bet those two were the winners of the strange expedition.

So remember, dear reader, whether you are discovering the wilderness of the far west and all of its wonders or simply voyaging to a house the next town over, navigation is a simple science that can get you where you want to go and back again. Learning the basics will give you understanding and confidence so you'll never be truly lost again.

# NAVIGATION NOTEBOOK

This book contains three types of forms that will help you in your basic exercises and on cross-country trips and voyages. Also, you will find the equipment checklist helpful in remembering what to bring and inspect before leaving.

## BASIC EXERCISES FORM

Objective:

Departing from:

Distance:

Magnetic course _____ Degrees

Return course _____ Degrees

Departure time:

Arrival time:

Check-point:

Check-point:

Check-point:

Check-point:

Compass variation:

True course:

Speed:

*Notes:*

# CROSS-COUNTRY NAVIGATION FORM

Objective:                          Departing from:

Overall Distance:                   Departure time:

Mag. Course:                        Compass variation:

Distance:                           Time:

Checkpoints:

**1.**

**2.**

**3.**

**4.**

**5.**

**6.**

**7.**

**8.**

**9.**

**10.**

Total time:

*Notes:*

Direct course out of wilderness _____ to _____.

# EQUIPMENT LIST

1.                                        2.

3.                                        4.

5.                                        6.

7.                                        8.

9.                                        10.

11.                                       12.

13.                                       14.

15.                                       16.

17.                                       18.

19.                                       20.

21.                                       22.

23.                                       24.

25.                                       26.

27.                                       28.

29.                                       30.

*Notes:*



Nearest Police Location:                 Phone:

Ranger Station Location:                 Phone:

Car parked at:

Car make and model:                      Plate No:

In case of emergency, call:

# MARINE NAVIGATION FORM

| Check-point | Mag. Course | Distance | Time | Speed |
|---|---|---|---|---|
| | To / Return | | | |
| 1. | / | | | |
| 2. | / | | | |
| 3. | / | | | |
| 4. | / | | | |
| 5. | / | | | |
| 6. | / | | | |
| 7. | / | | | |
| 8. | / | | | |
| 9. | / | | | |
| 10. | / | | | |

Tachometer Setting:                    Emergency Radio Channels:

Speedometer Reading:                  Weather Channel:

ETA:

ATA:

Tide:

Current:

*Notes:*

## BOATMAN'S CHECKLIST

1. Fuel
2. Spare fuel
3. Oil
4. Spare oil
5. Fresh, potable water
6. Battery
7. Spare battery
8. Jumper cables
9. Stuffing box
10. Hose clamps
11. Transmission oil
12. Water pump drive belts
13. Spare spark plugs
14. Shire pins
15. Spare prop
16. Bilge
17. Blower
18. Bilge pump
19. Switches
20. Fuel filters
21. Steering
22. Lights
23. Horn
24. Radio
25. Depth finder
26. Life jackets
27. First-aid kit
28. Ring buoy with line
29. Flares
30. Flashlight
31. Towing line
32. Bucket
33. Binoculars
34. Charts
35. Compass
36. Spare compass
37. Paddle
38. Sunglasses
39. Tools
40. Fire extinguishers
41. Copy of rules of road

# FURTHER READING

For those interested in a complete text on small boat navigation, I recommend Charles F. Chapman's Piloting Seamanship and Small Boat Handling (published by Hearst Books, New York, and revised from time to time). This is one of the most comprehensive and best written books ever printed on the subject.

Other recommended books on advanced navigation and seamanship are:

Dunlap, G.D. & Shufeldt, Capt. H. H. (1972). *Dutton's Navigation and Piloting, 12*[th] *Edition*. Annapolis, MD: Naval Institute Press.

Von, Dorn, William J. (1974). *Oceanography and Seamanship*. New York, NY: Dodd Mead.

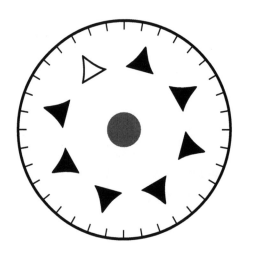

# INDEX

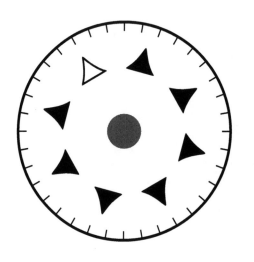

# ABOUT THE AUTHOR

Captain Robert R. Singleton, PhD is a merchant marine captain and an-oceanographer who has spent well over 40 years at sea. He is also aprivate pilot and an ex-paratrooper from the famed 101st AirborneDivision. Captain Singleton has authored several books and other articles,including "You'll Never Get Lost Again: Simple Navigation for Everyone,""The Standish Chronicles," and "Angels, Visions, and Gifts." He enjoyswriting, teaching, and many outdoor activities.

Made in the USA
Columbia, SC
01 May 2019

TRA008000    TRANSPORTATION / Navigation
SPO036000    SPORTS & RECREATION / Sailing                                    $19
REF015000    REFERENCE / Personal & Practical Guides                          L1

Imagine you're on a road trip somewhere in the middle of nowhere—no towns for miles, it's nighttime, and there is no cell service. Suddenly, your GPS fails. You didn't print out directions. All you have in your glove compartment is a map and a compass. What would you do?

Captain Robert R. Singleton explains the not-so-complicated science of simple navigation. Starting from the absolute basics, "You'll Never Get Lost Again" can teach even the most directionally-challenged how to find their way to any destination with little more than a compass, a map, and a sense of adventure.

This book uses simple, easy-to-understand instructions, real-life exercises, detailed diagrams, and straightforward explanations to guide any beginner to a better understanding of basic navigation while also reminding the advanced navigator of the importance of simple concepts in an important science.

By the time you've finished "You'll Never Get Lost Again", you'll have the confidence to know that, as long as you understand the basics, you can find your way to any destination in the world – from the grocery store around the block to the far reaches of the great-untamed wilderness.

*The world is yours for the navigating.*

## Atlantic Publishing Group, Inc.

Your complete resource for small business, management, finance, online, real estate, and young adult books covering subjects such as careers, college life, education, finance, history, lifestyle, and writing.
*We have a book for that.*™

1405 SW 6th Ave • Ocala, FL 34471-0640
Phone 352-622-1825 • Fax 352-622-1875
www.atlantic-pub.com

ISBN-13: 9781620235904

51995

9 781620 235904